"This book is dedicated to all who find joy and peace in the colors of life. May each page bring a moment of calm and creativity, brightening your days as colors brighten the world. With love and affection...

Roberto C Bezerra

Jan/2024

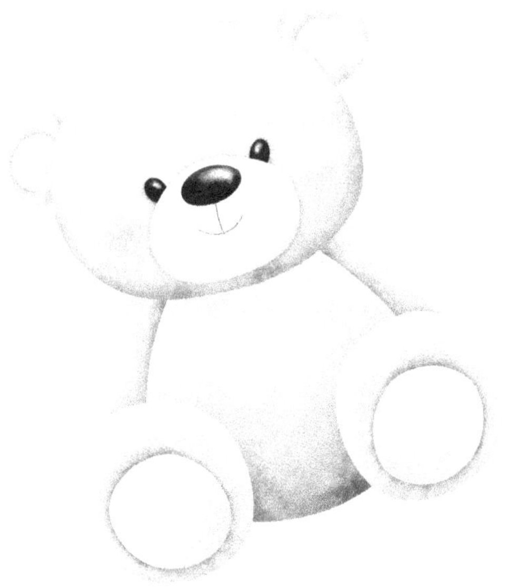
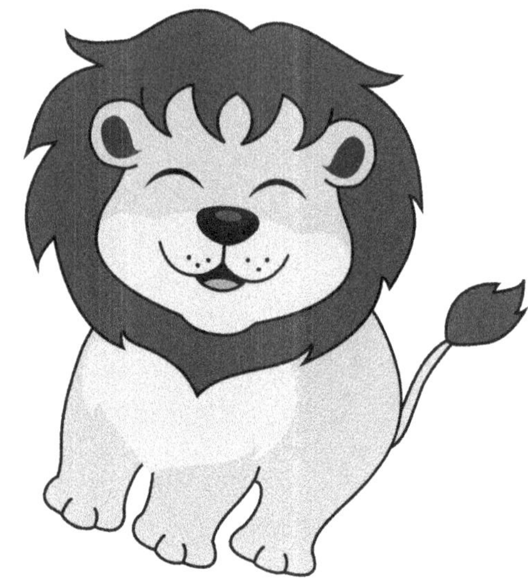

This Book Belongs to:

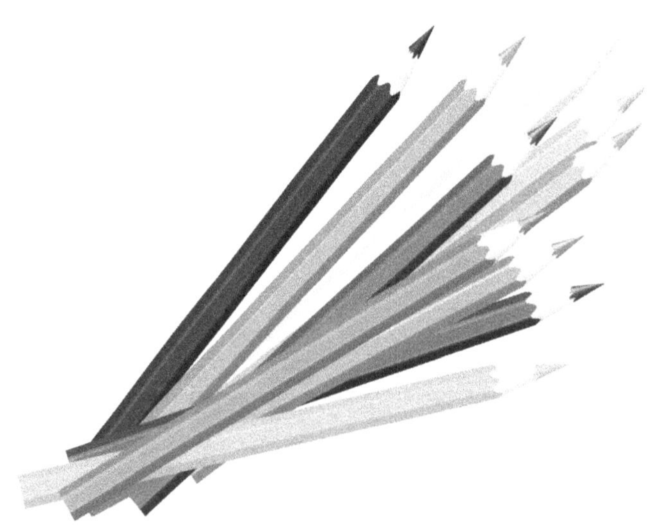

Test Color Page

Peacock

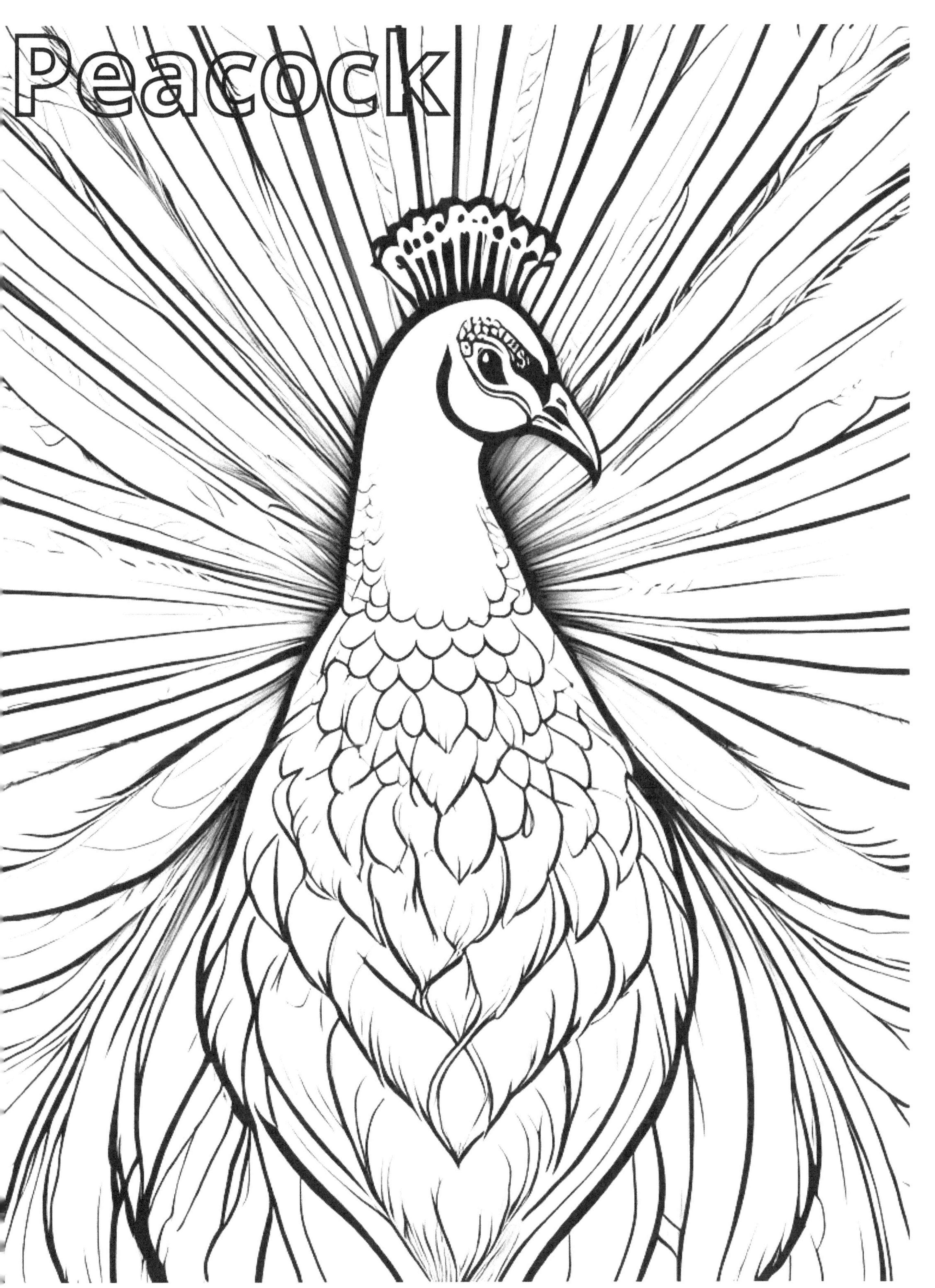

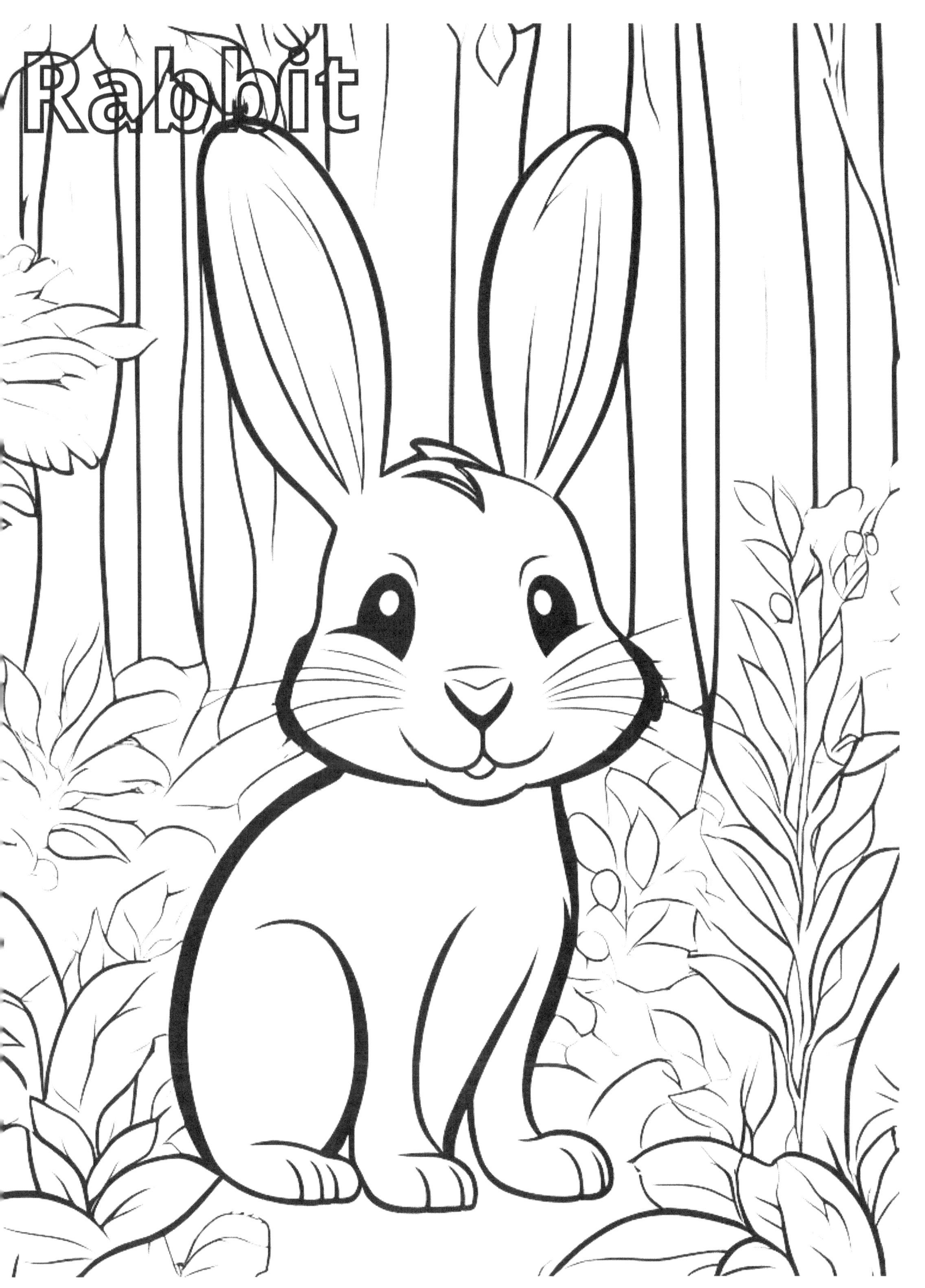
Rabbit

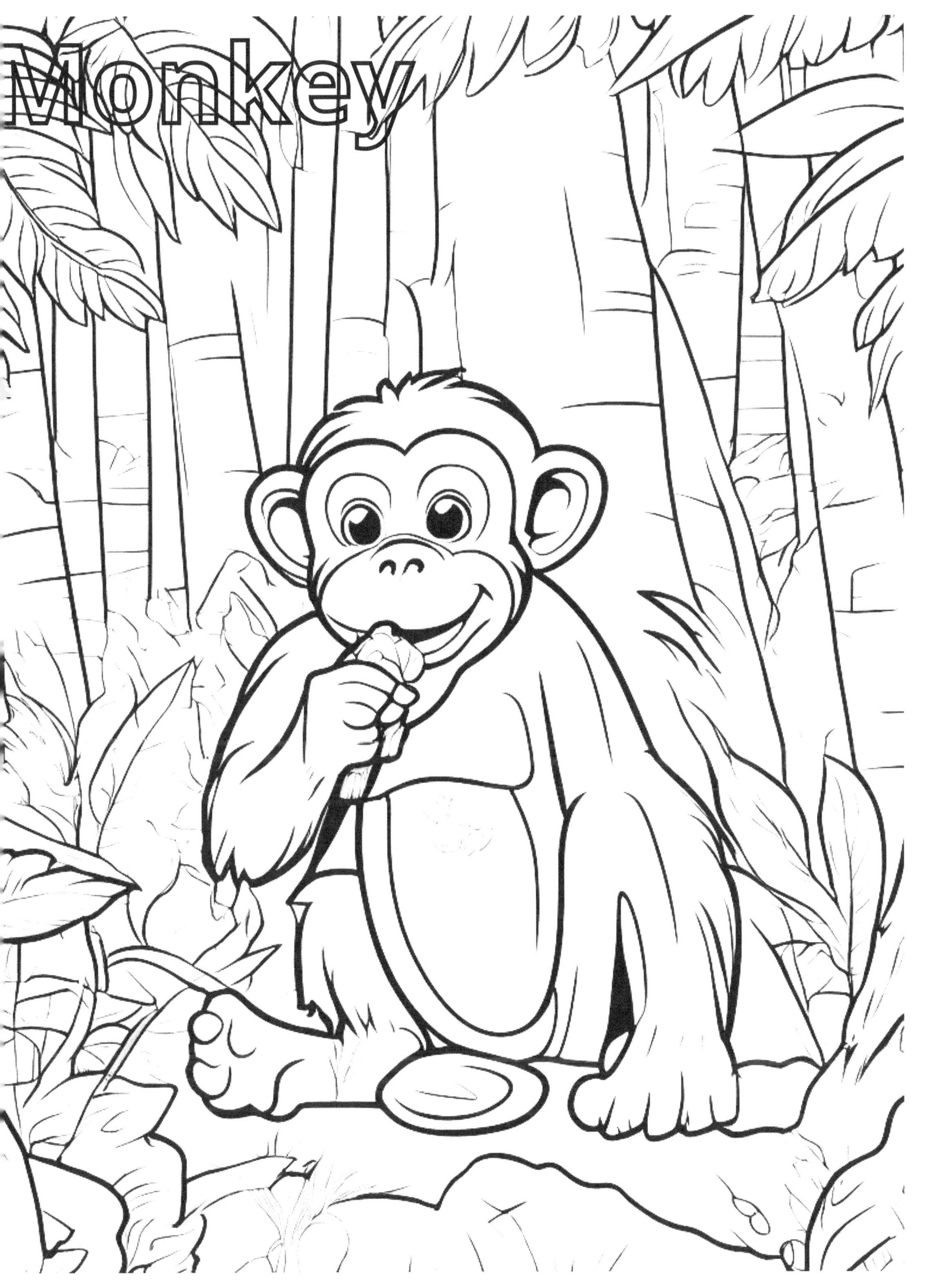

Monkey

Lion

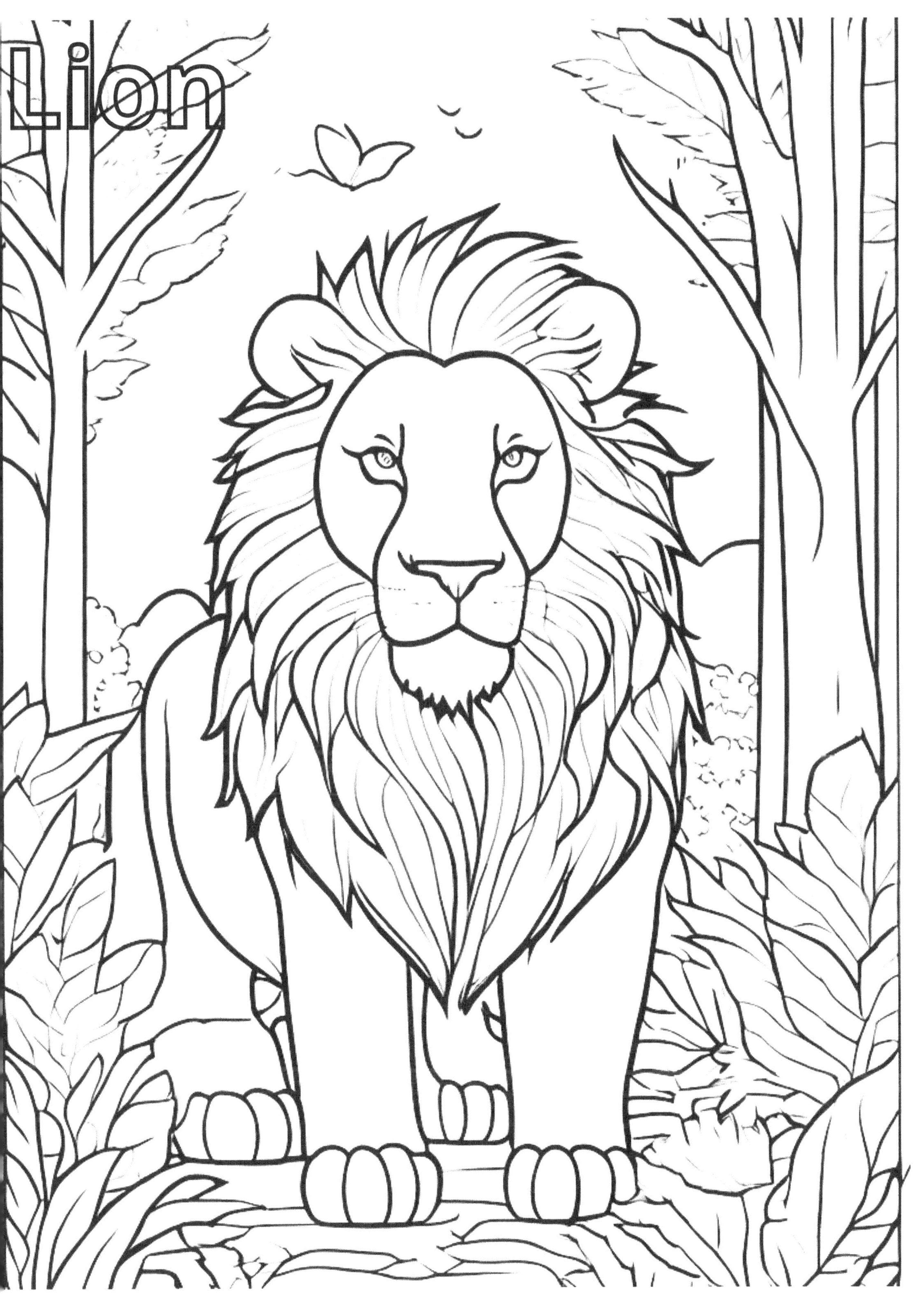

Horse

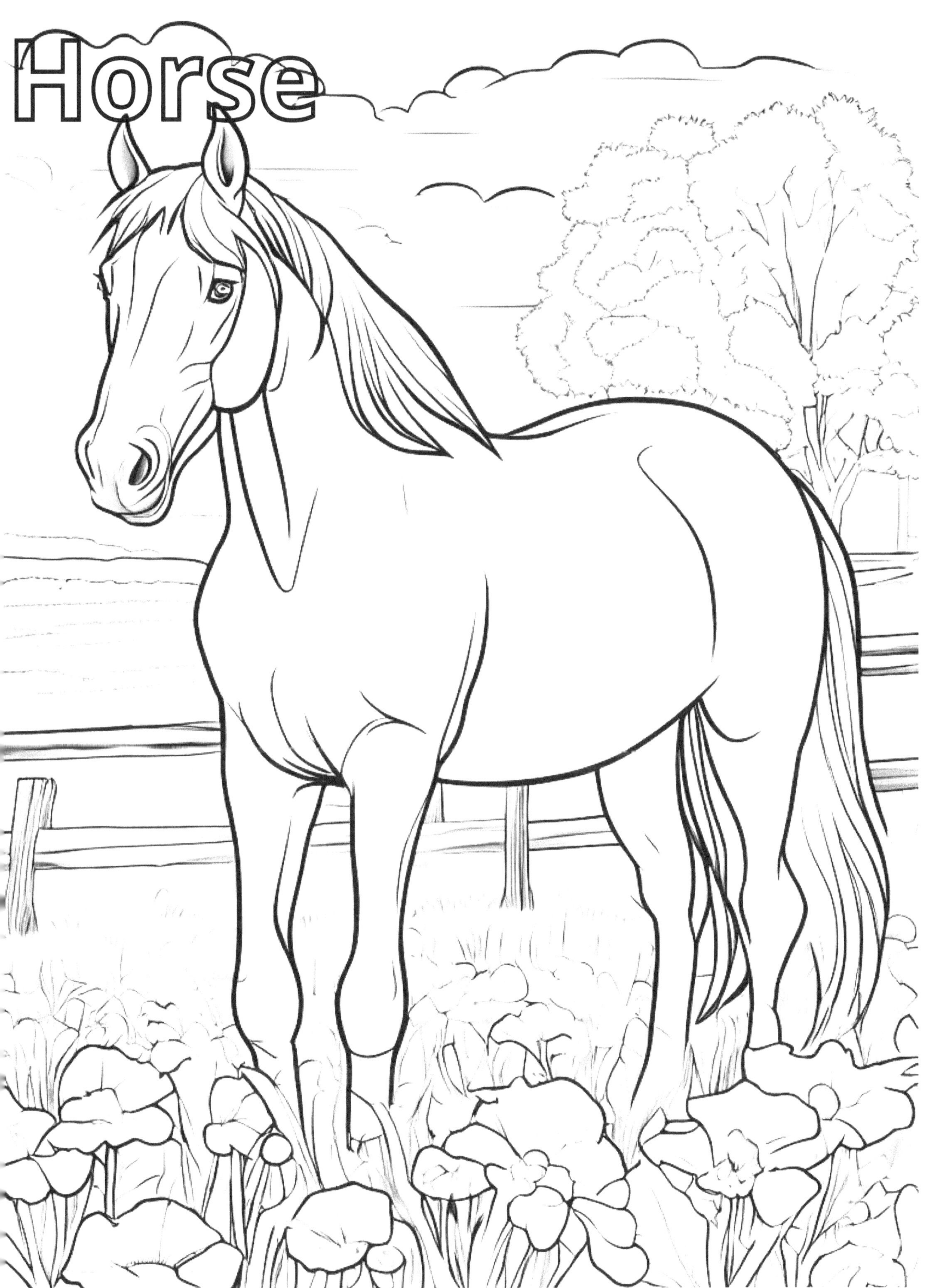

Jaguar

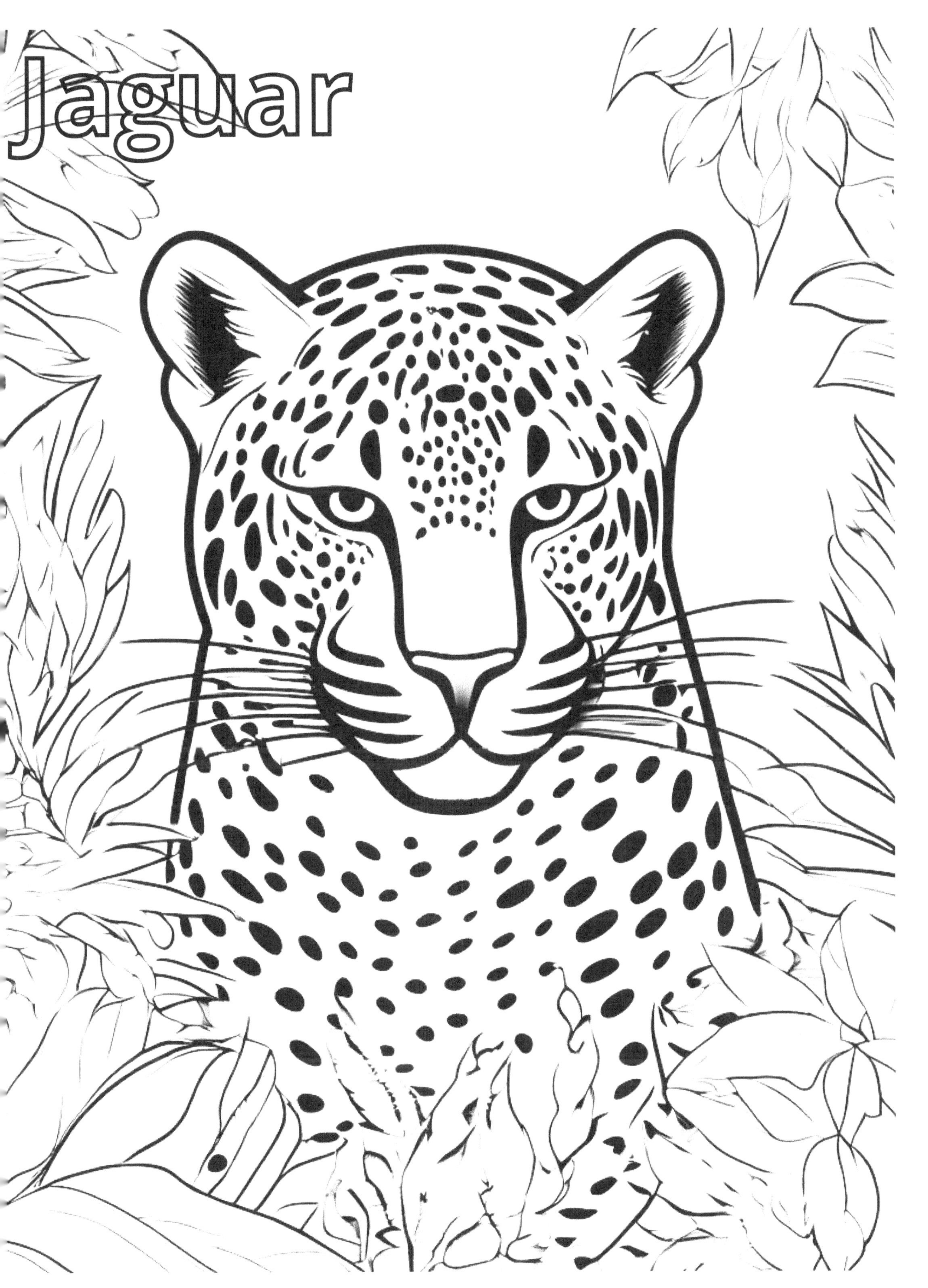

Hen

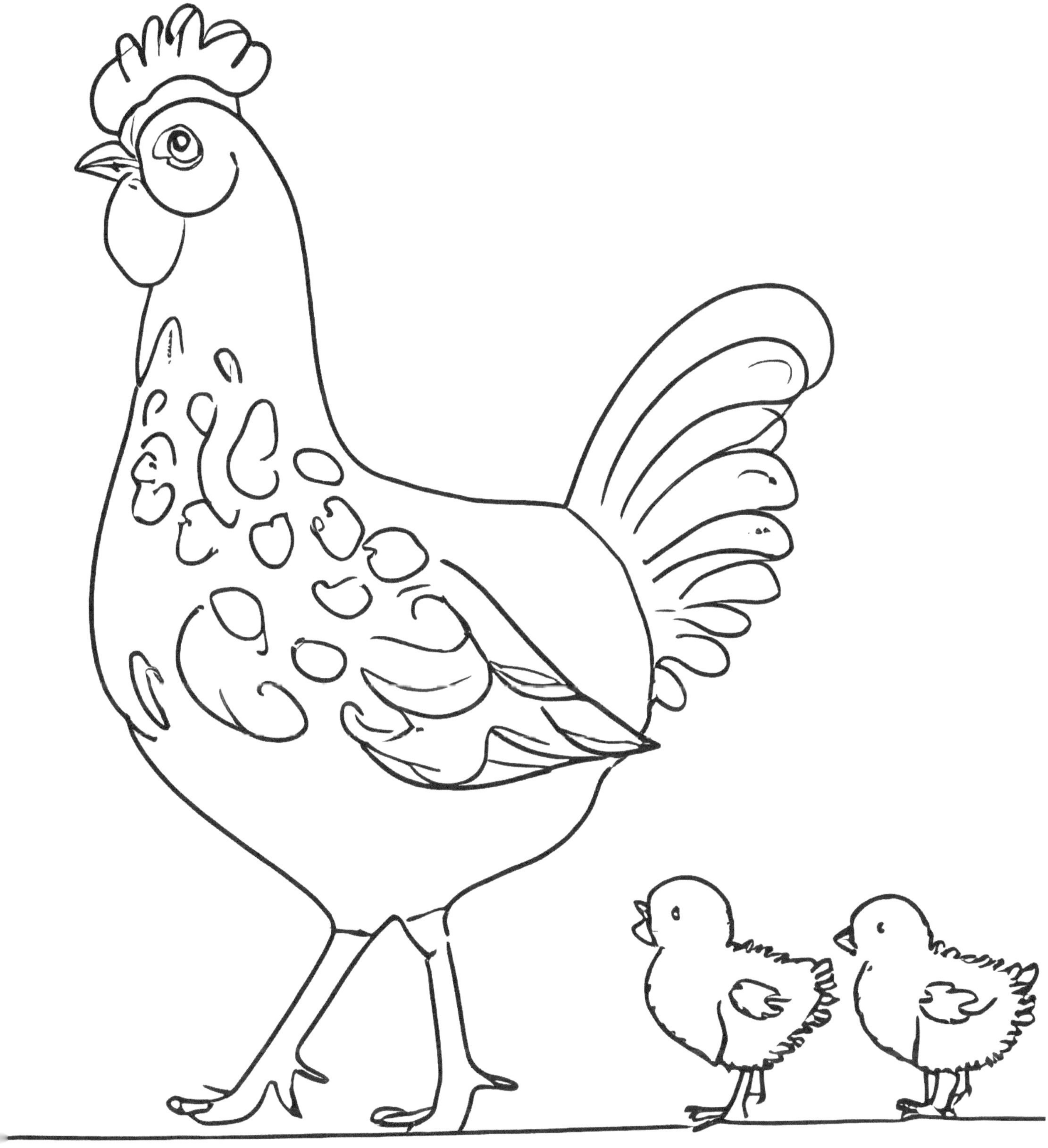

Guinea pig

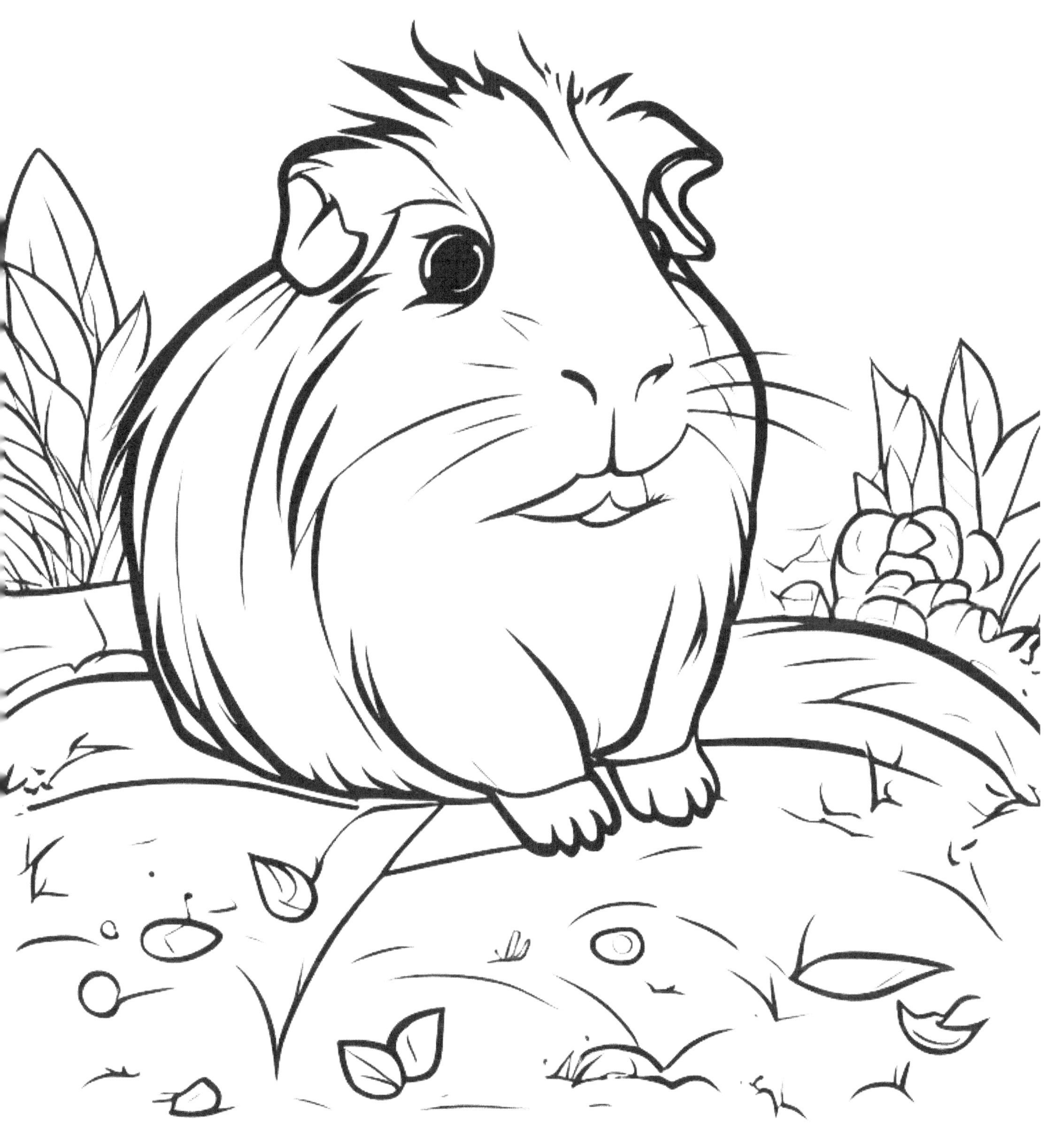

Frog

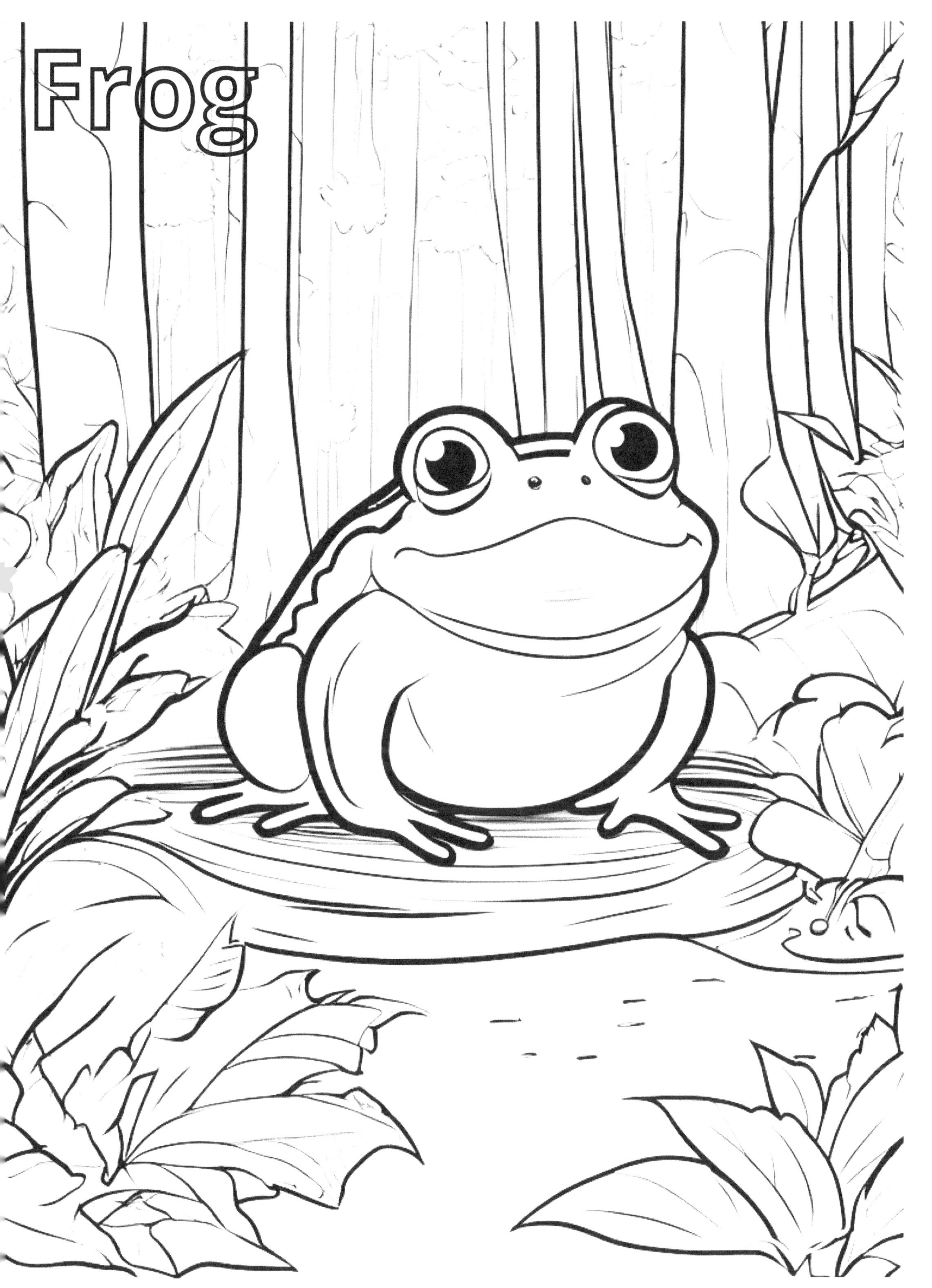

widgeon

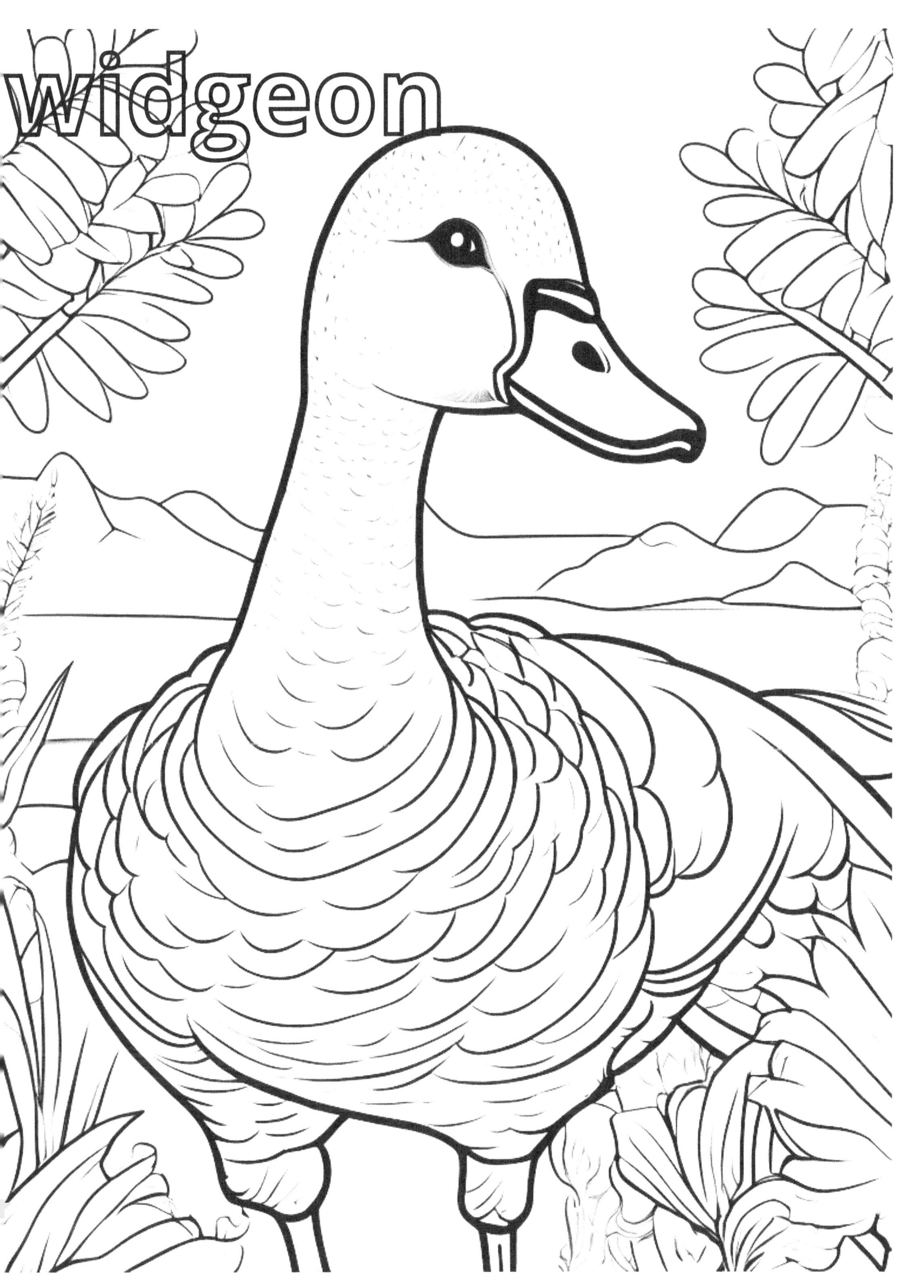

Fox

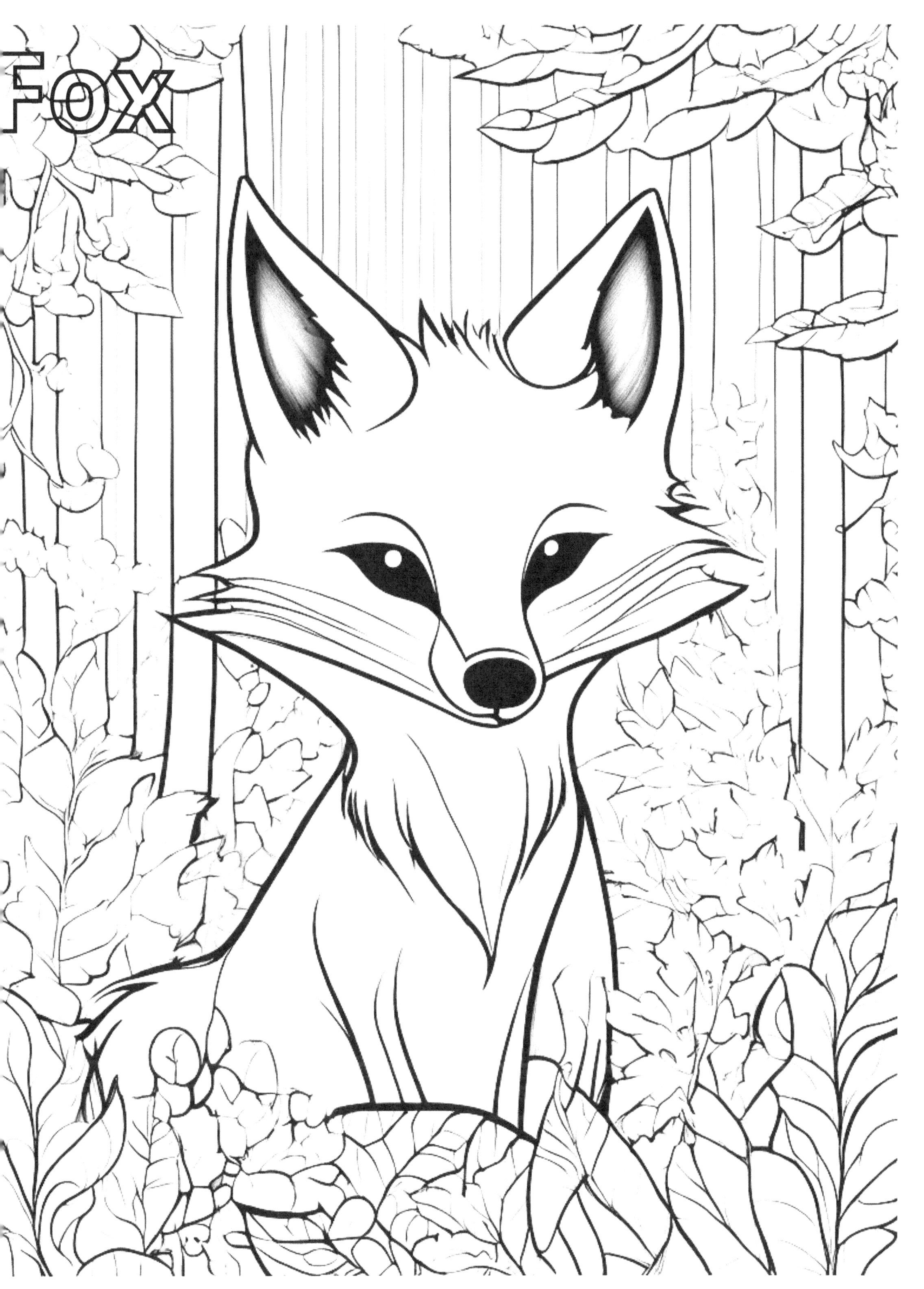

Elefant

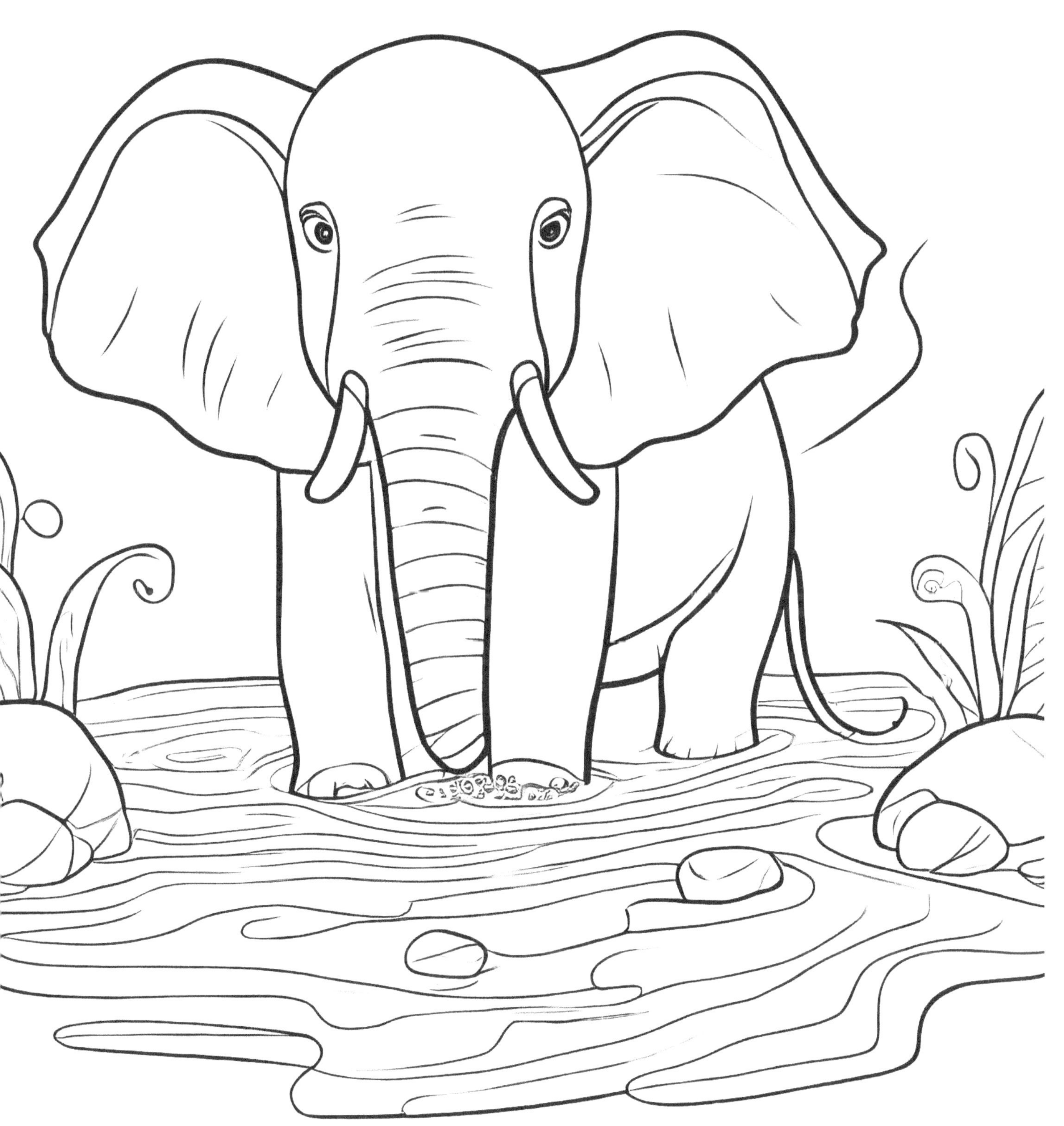

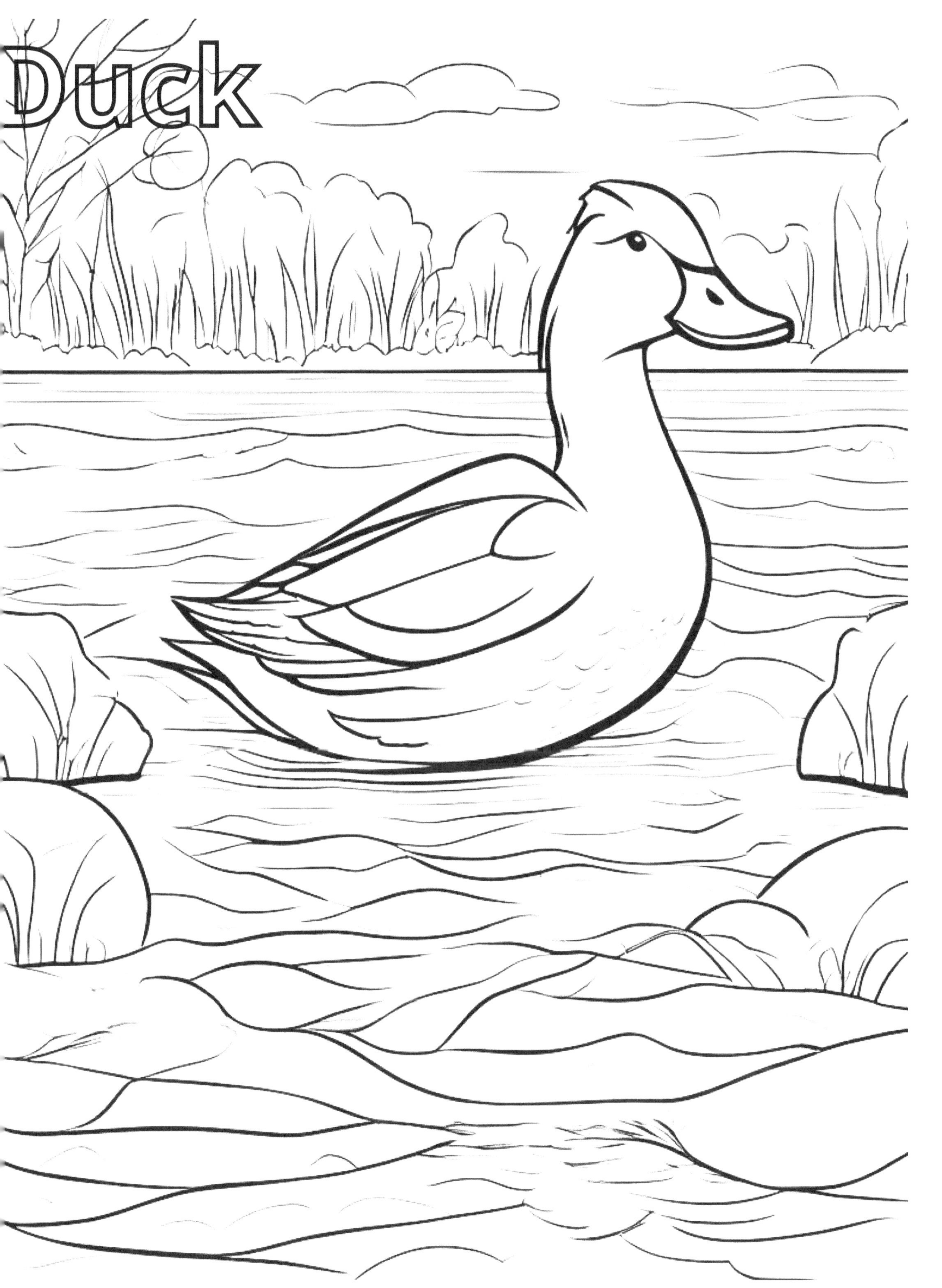

Duck

Alligator

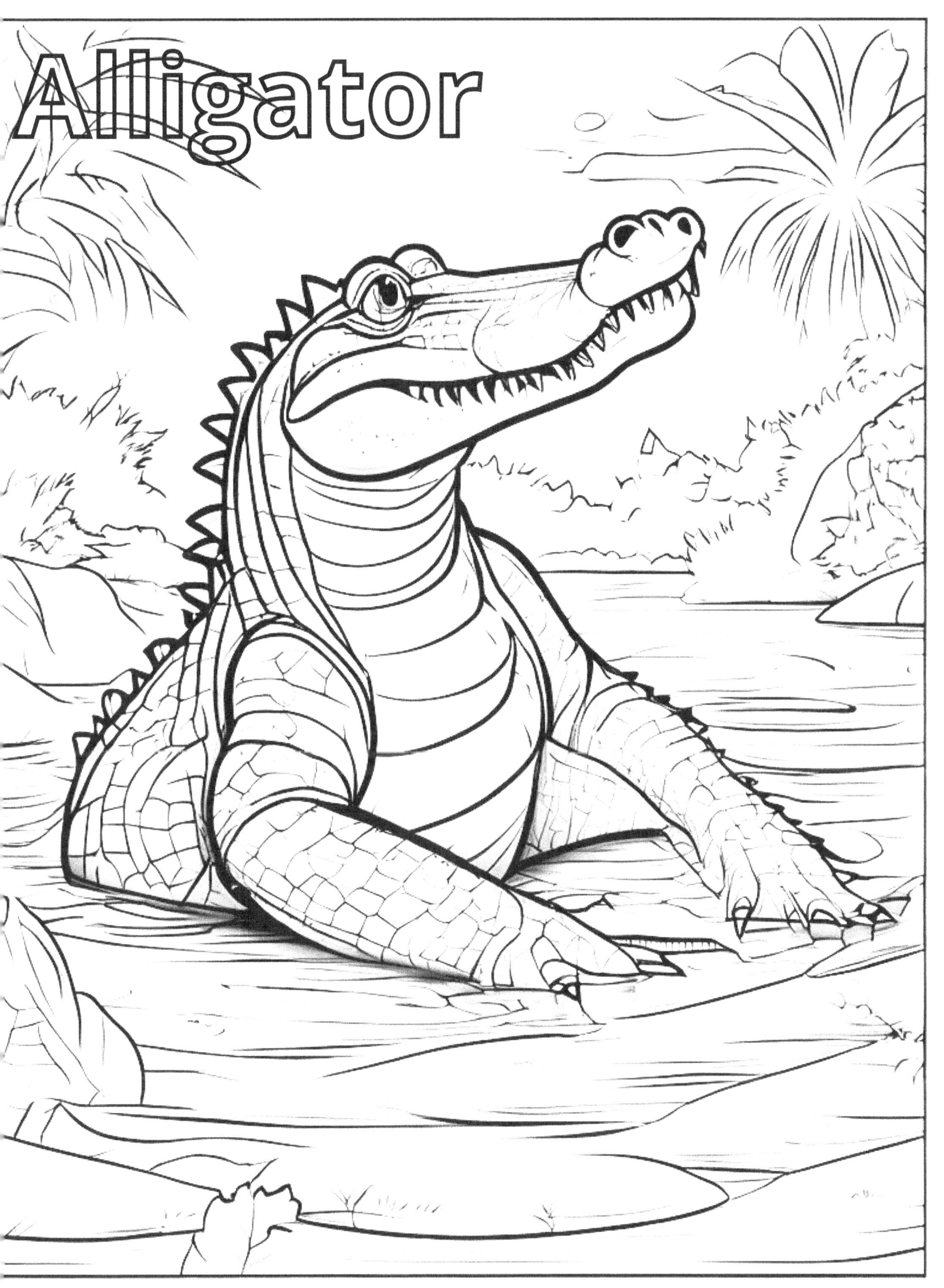

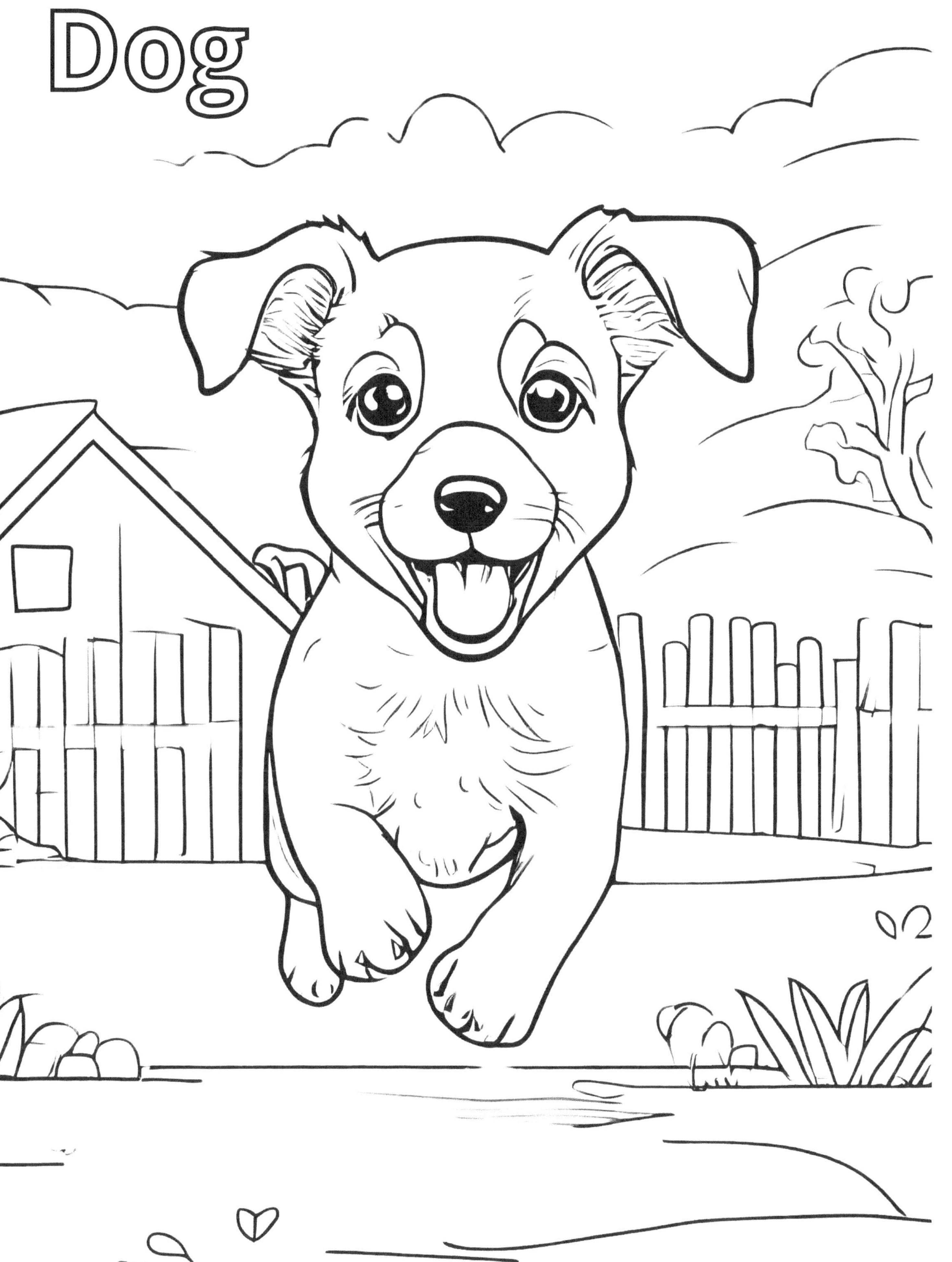

Dog

Cow

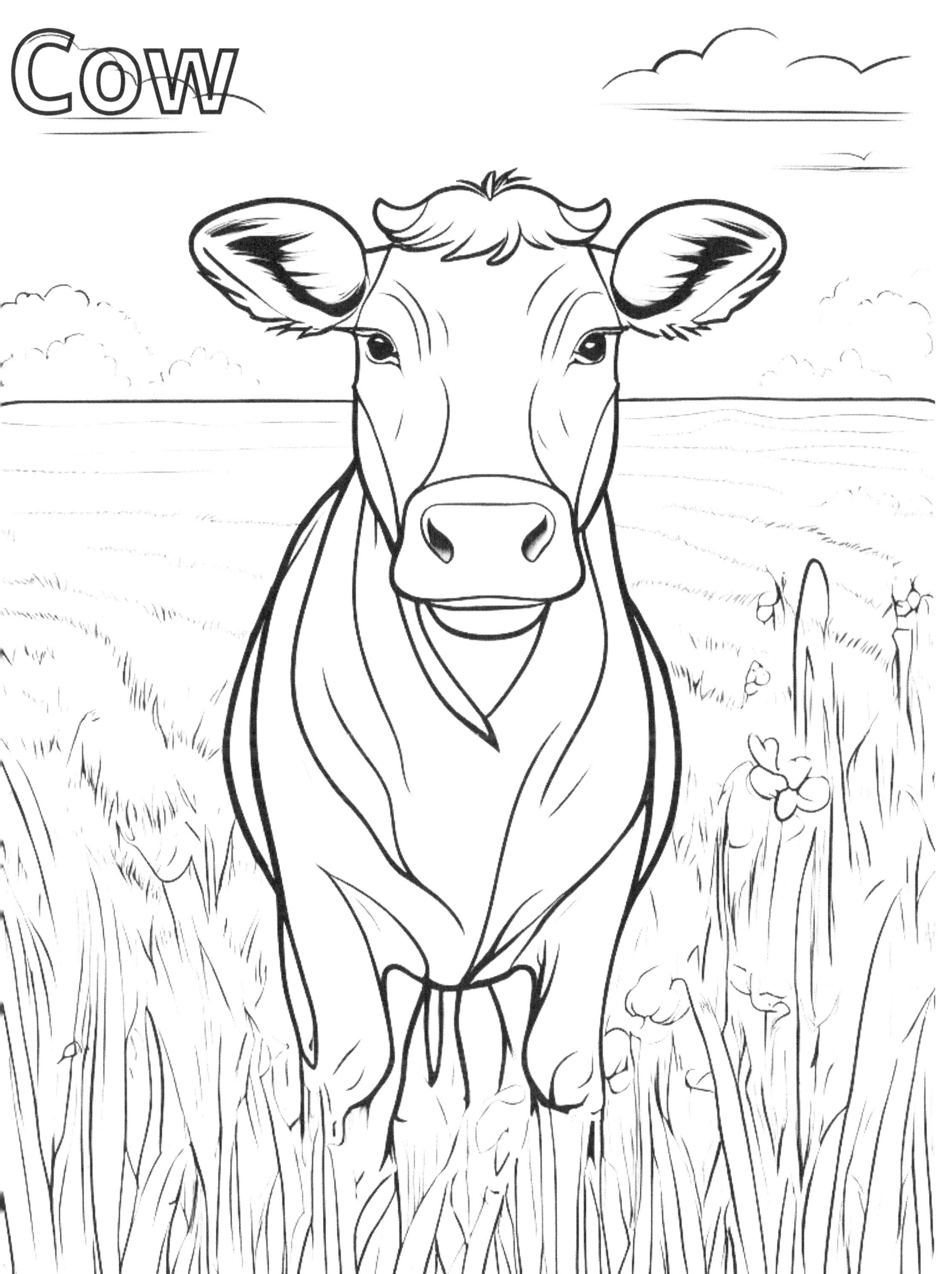

Cat

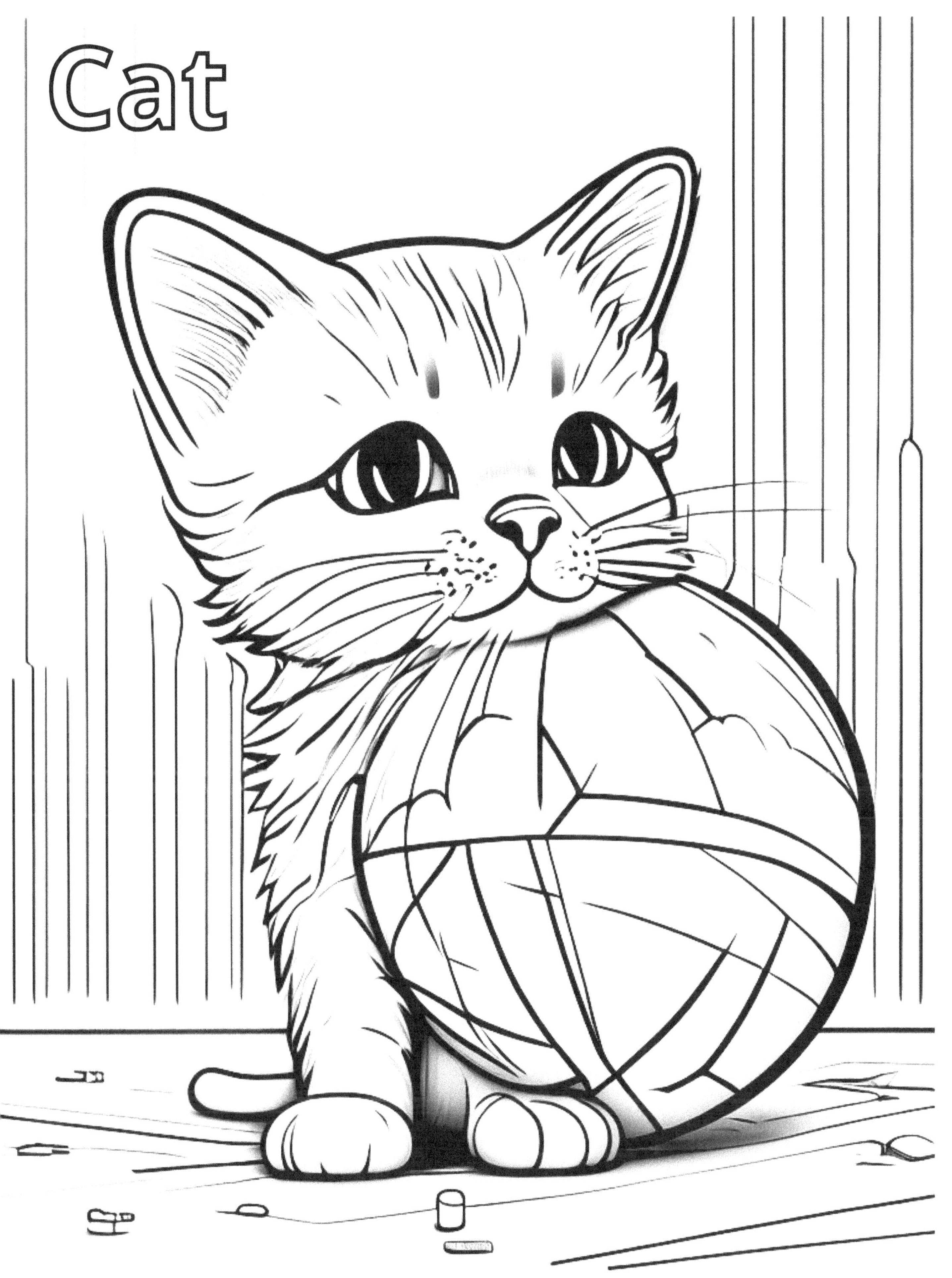

Anteater

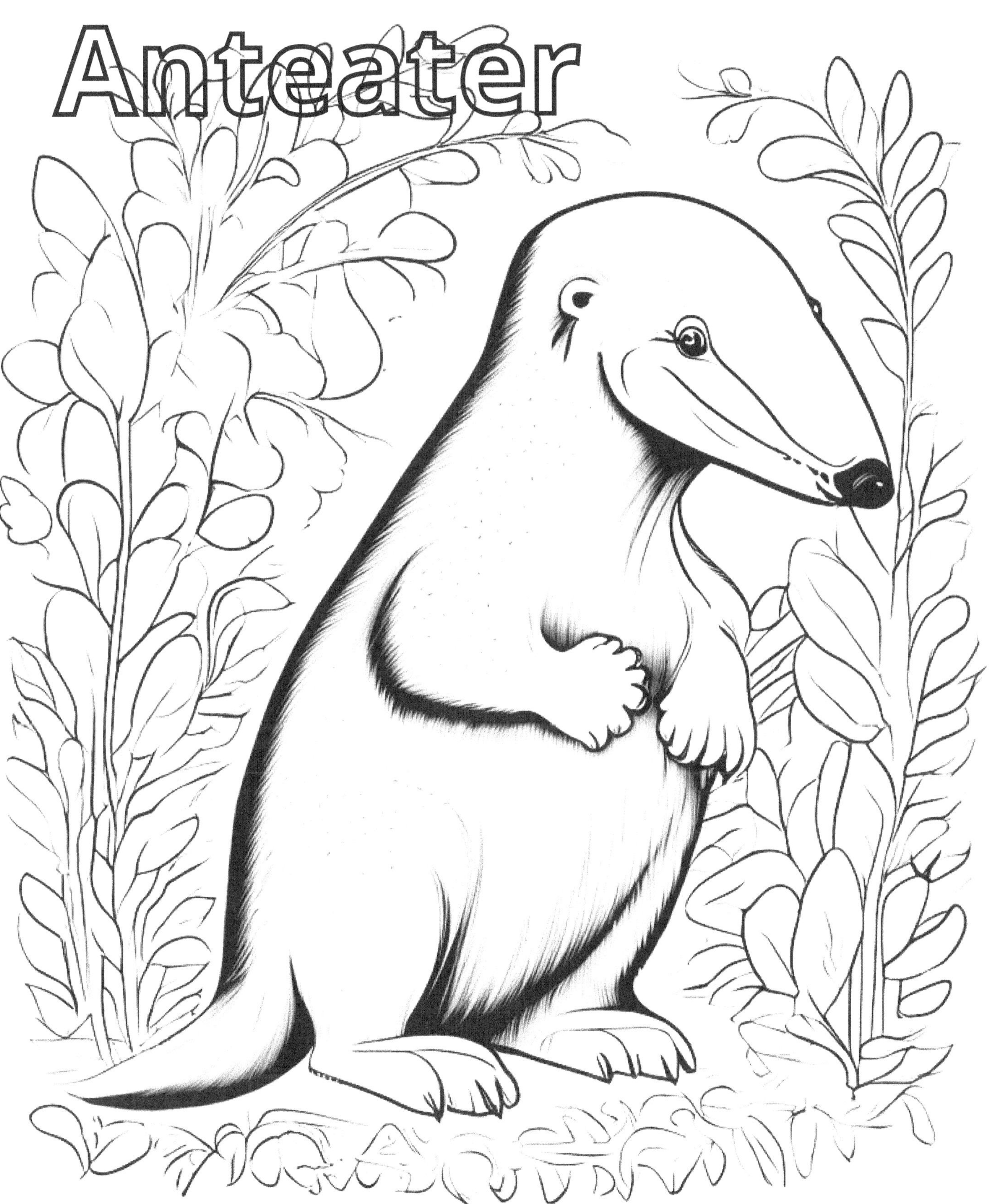

Bear

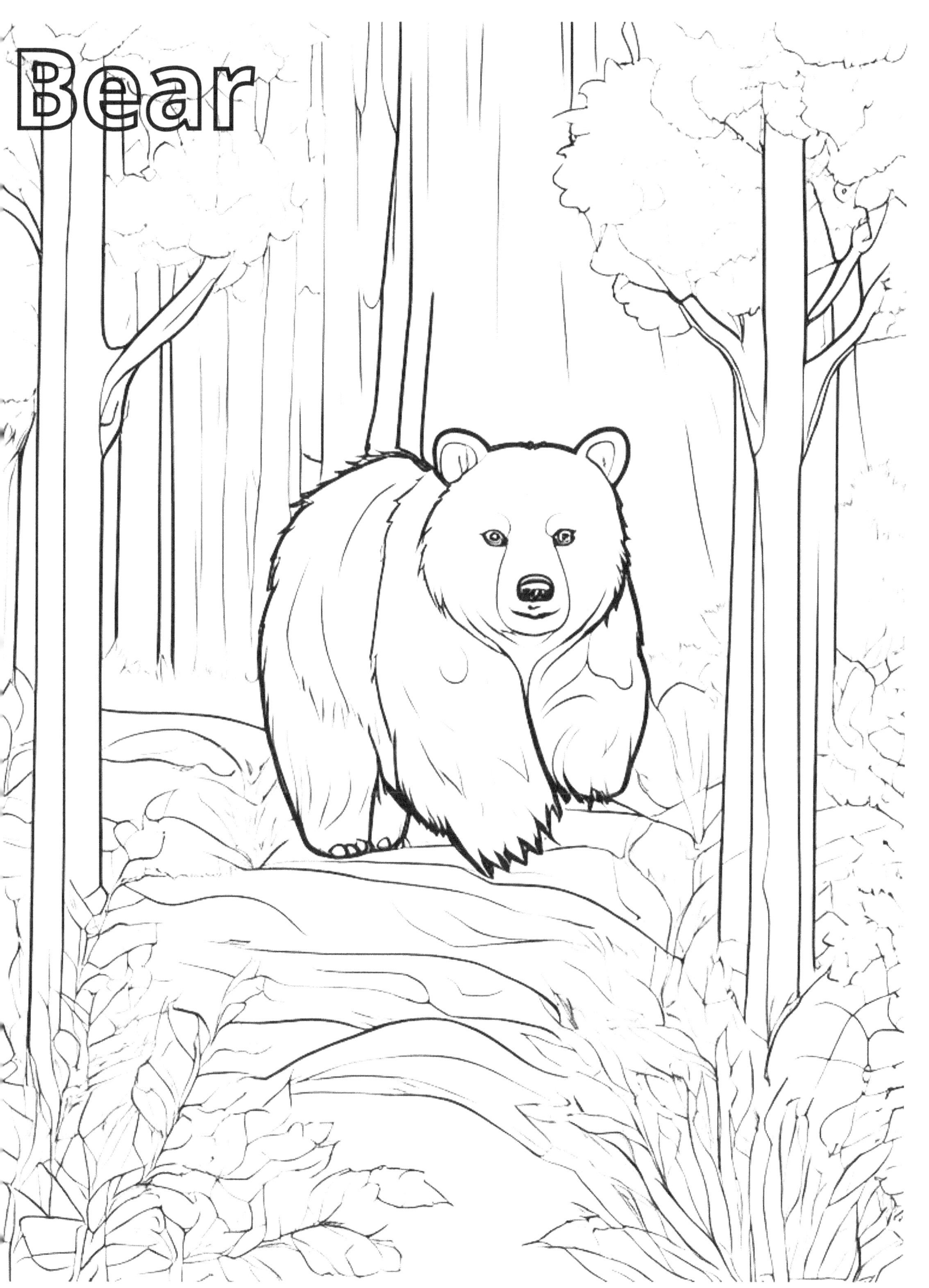

Dog

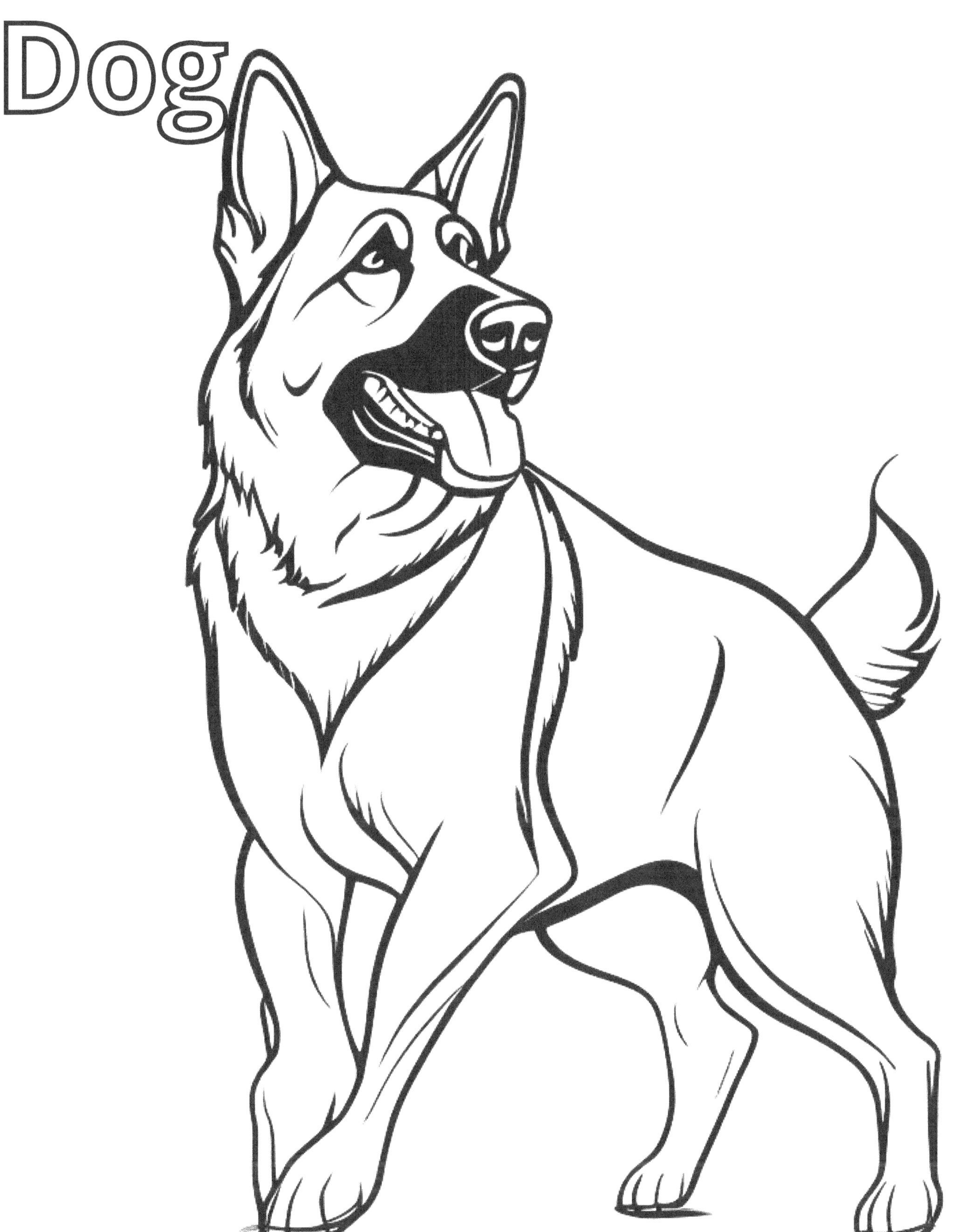

Cat

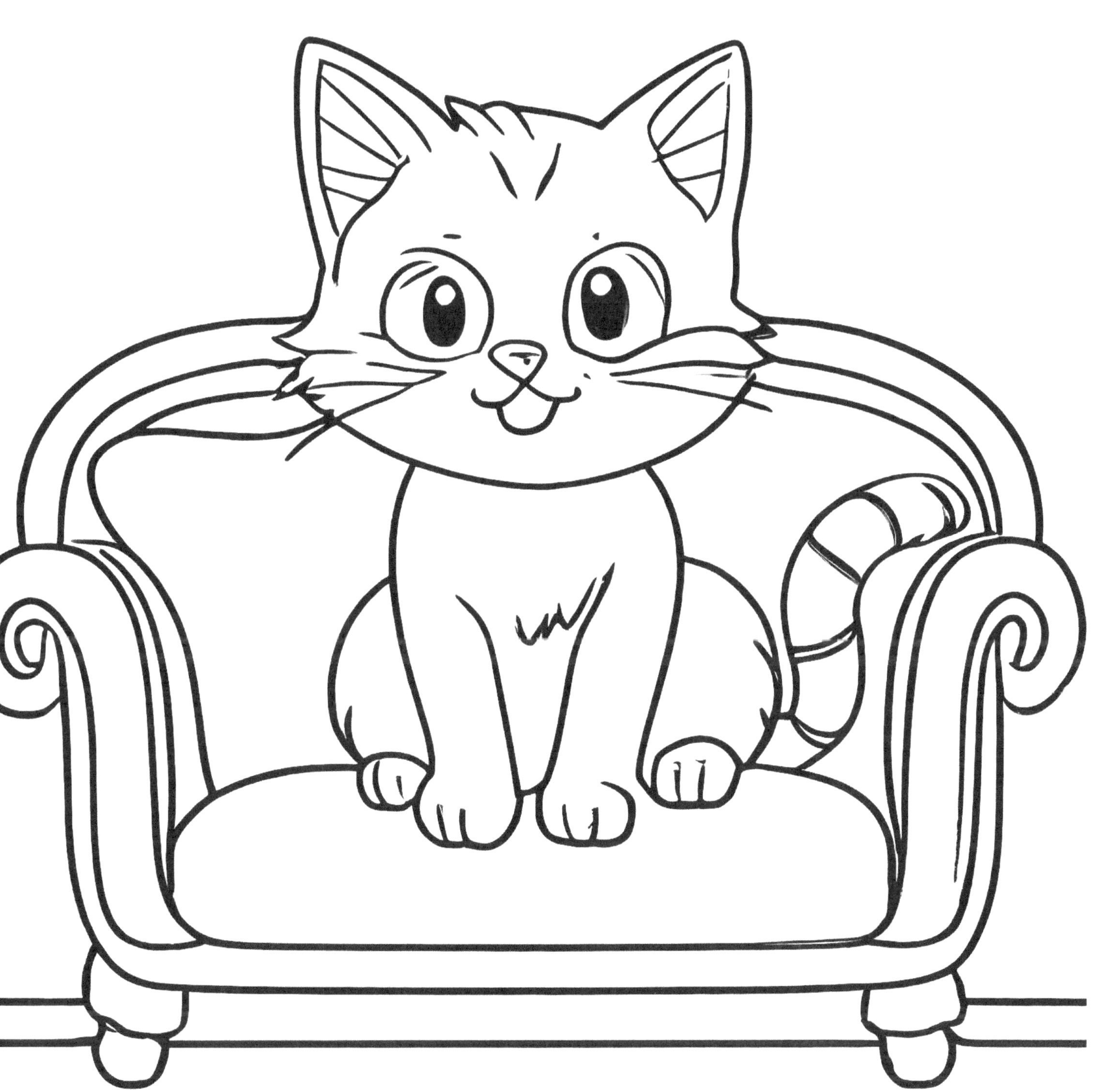

Parrot

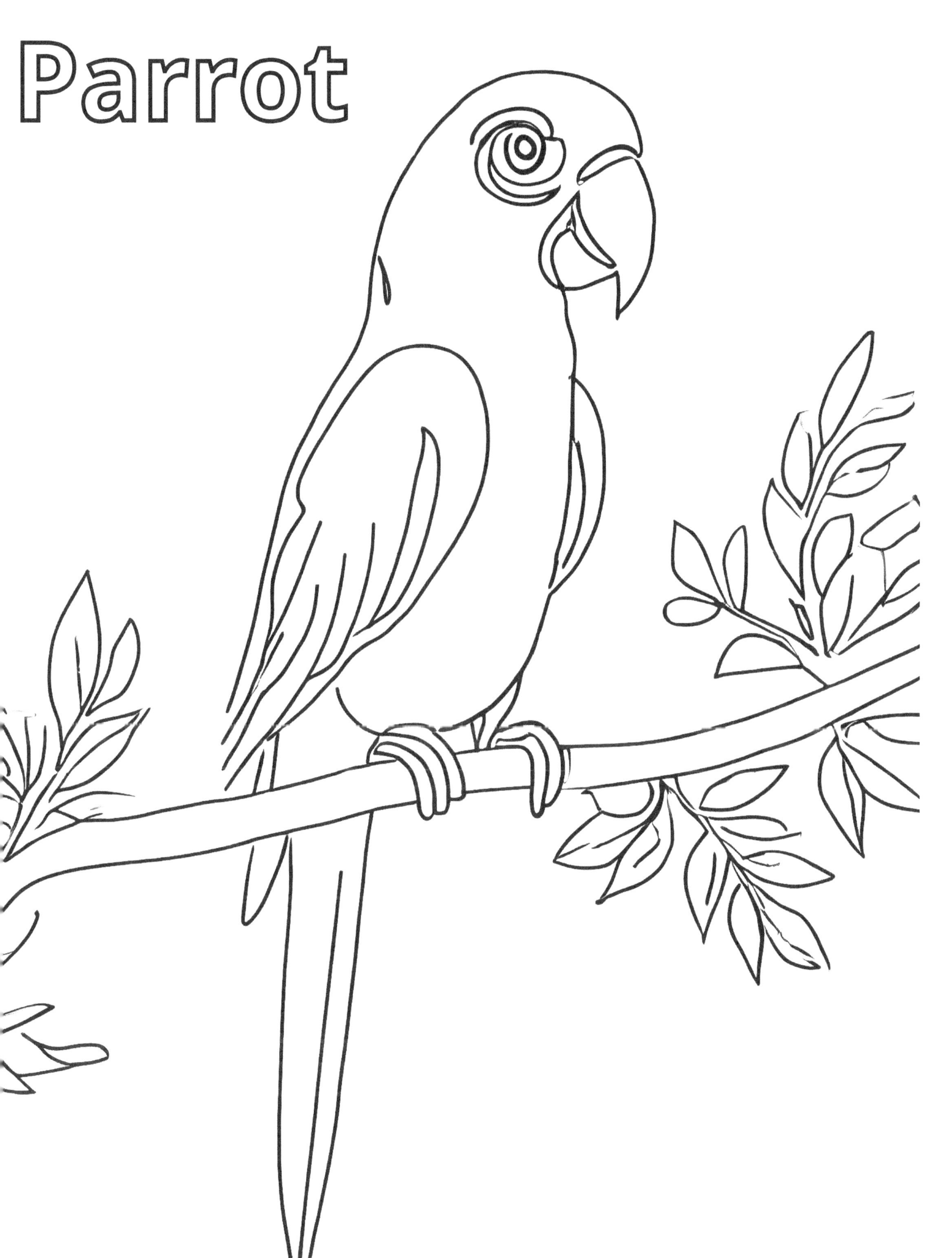

Dolphin

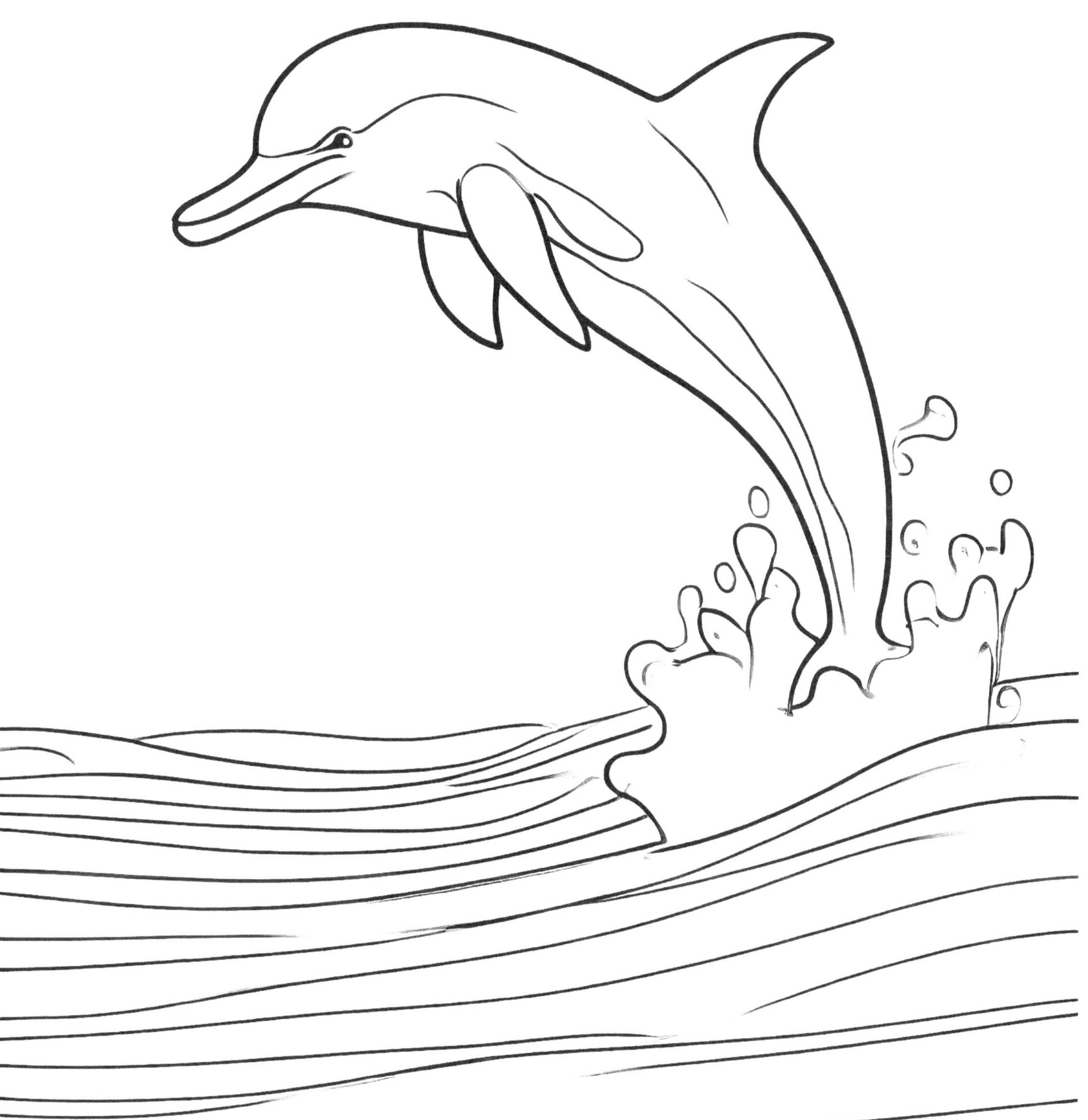

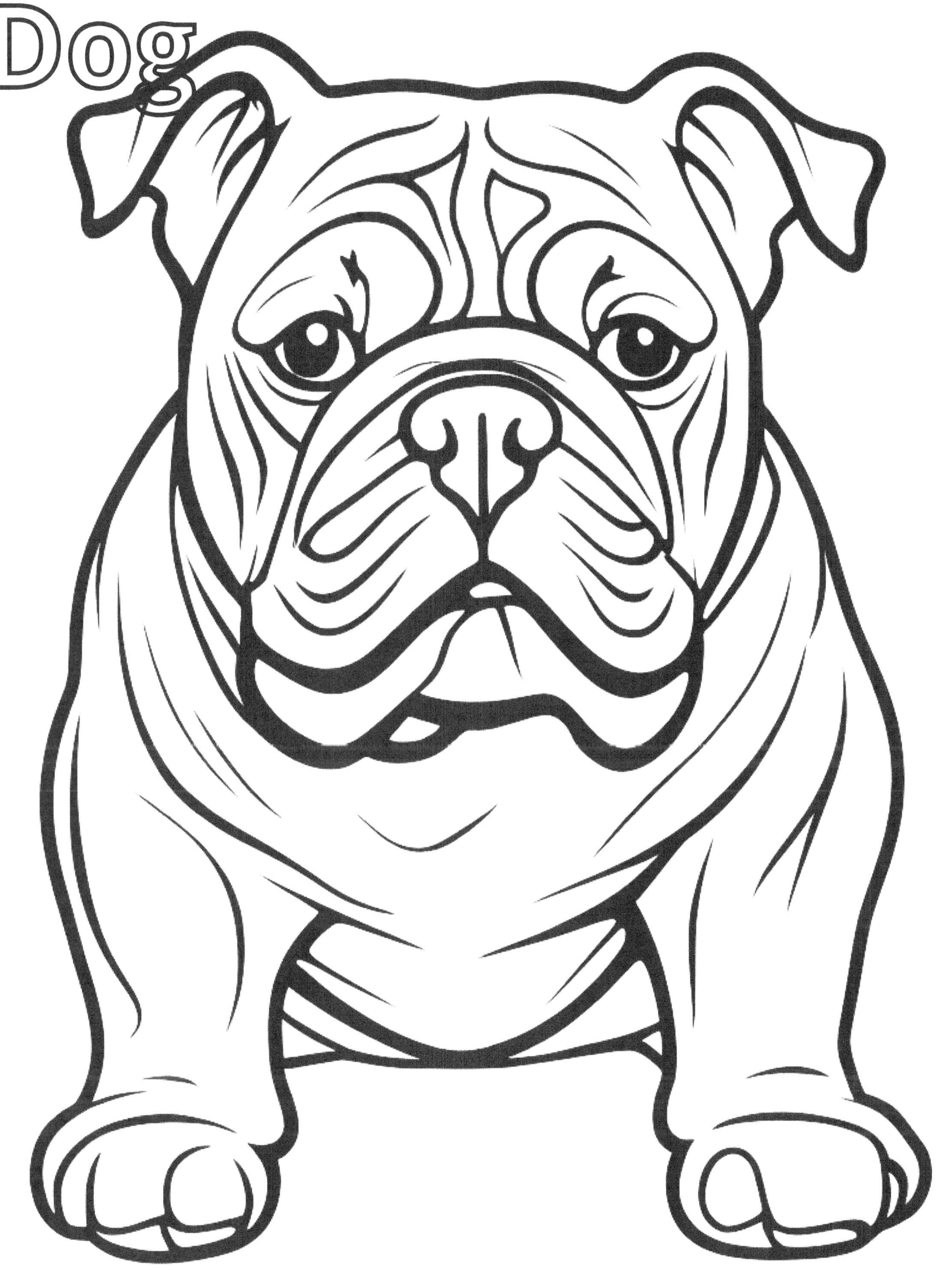
Dog

Ostrich

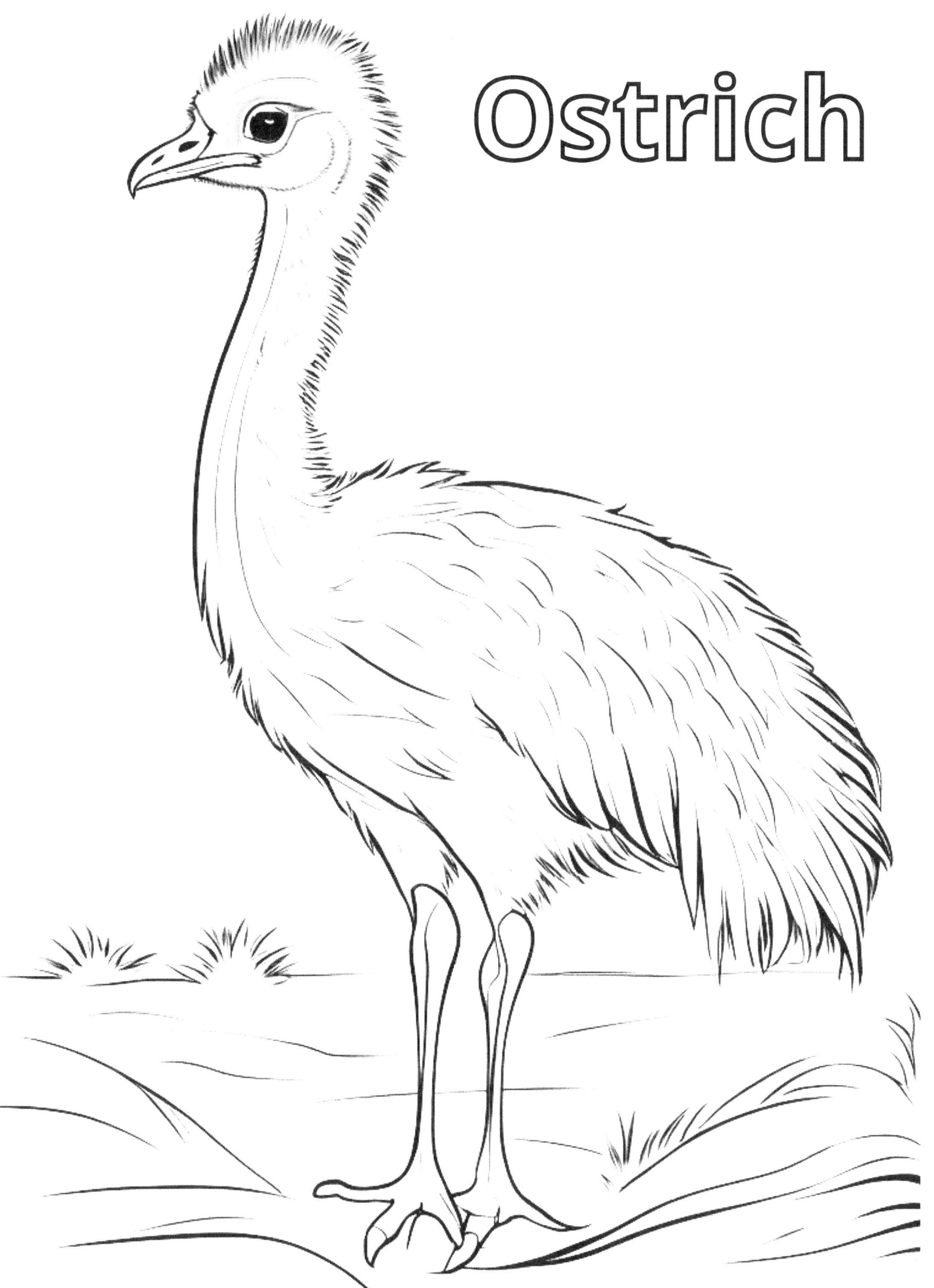

Monkey

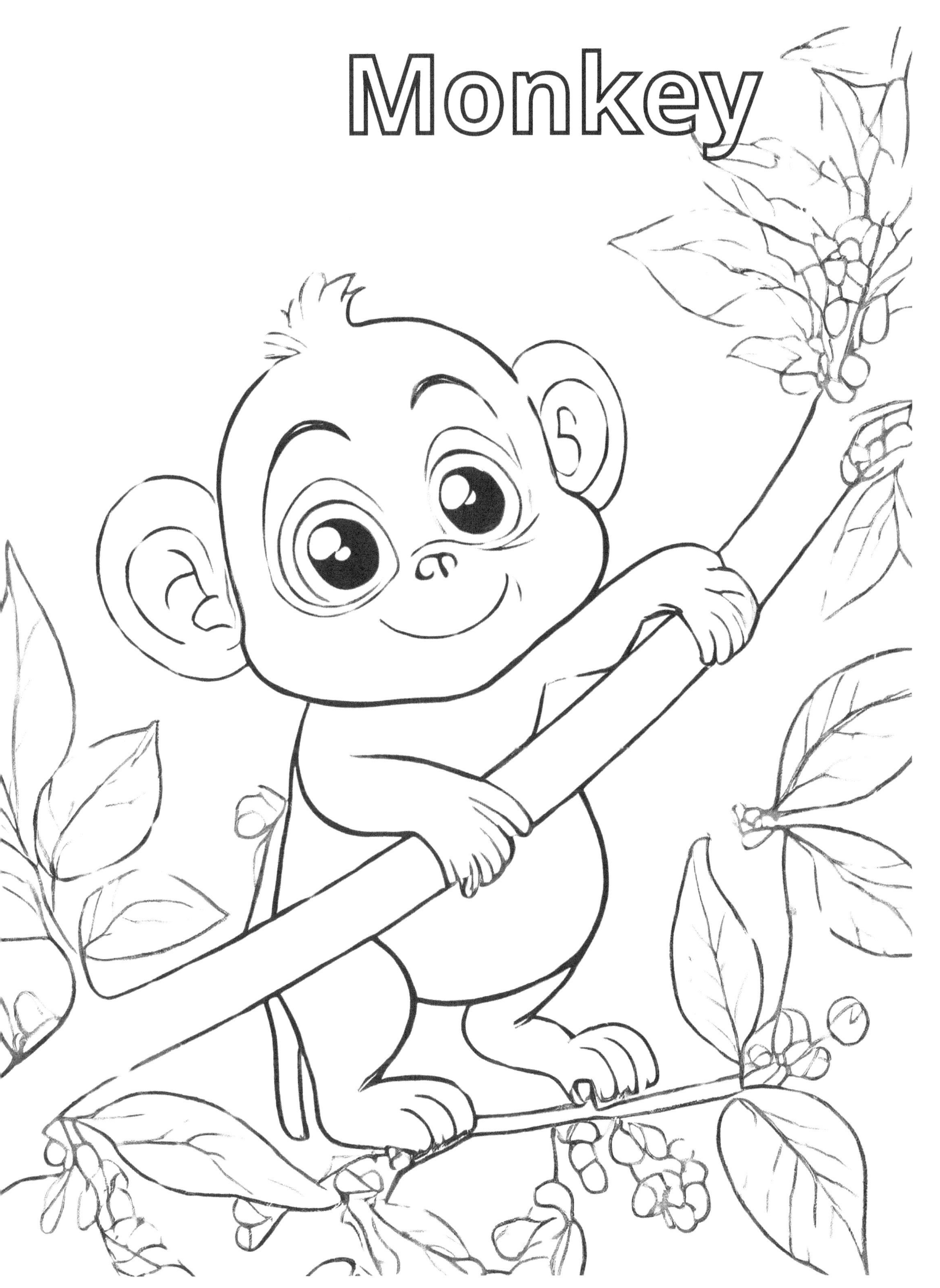

Owl

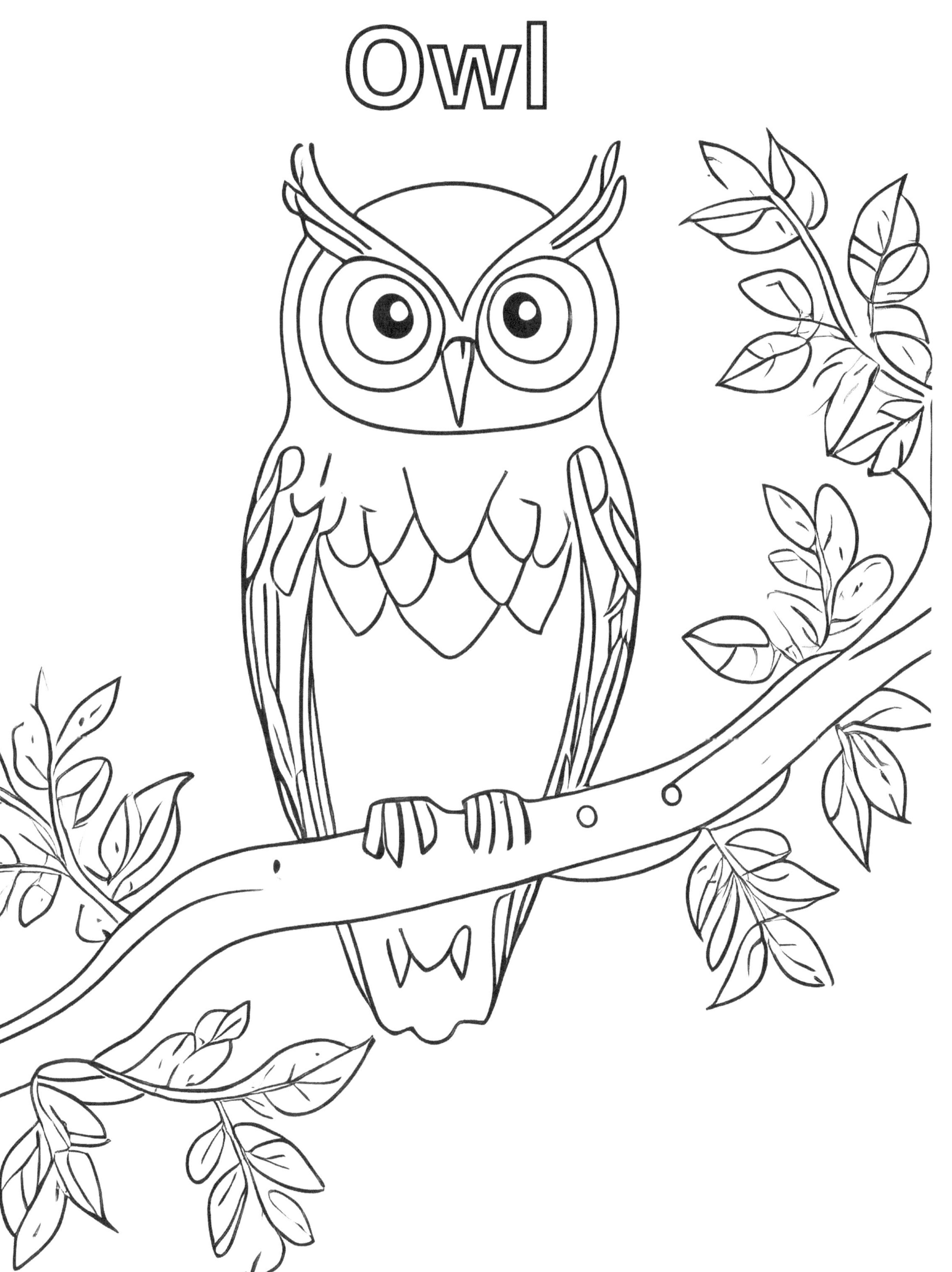

Hummingbird

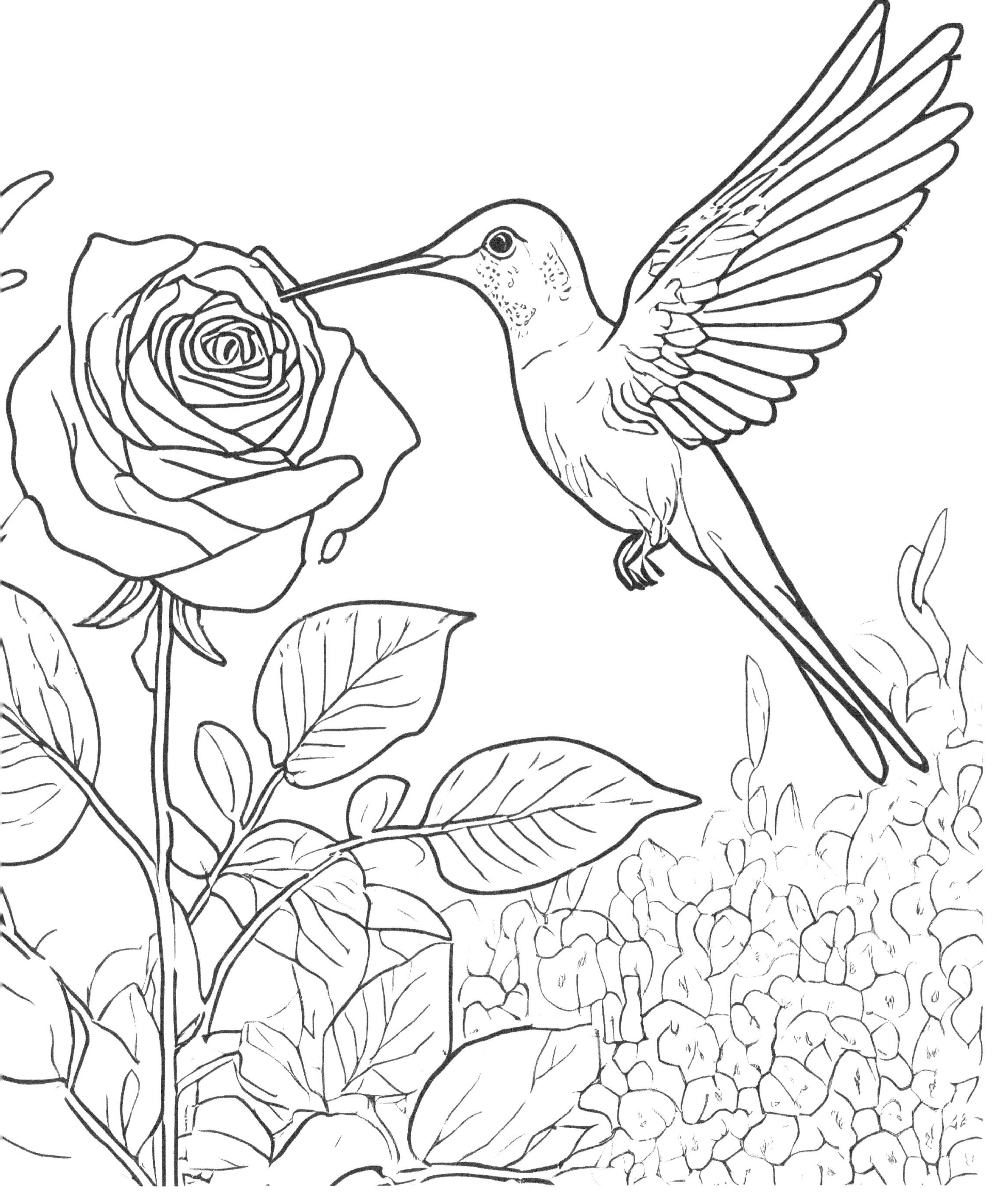

Mouse

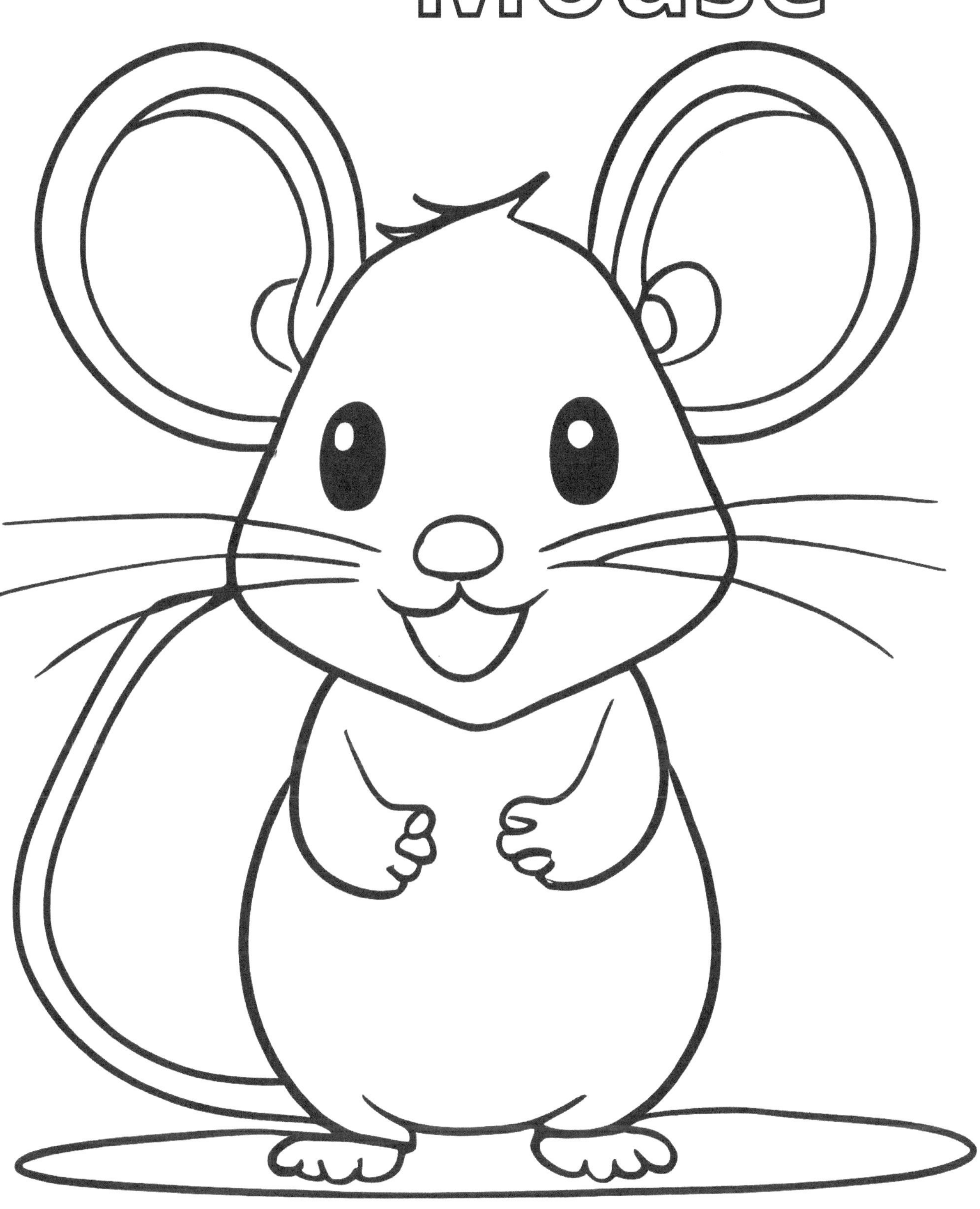

Deer

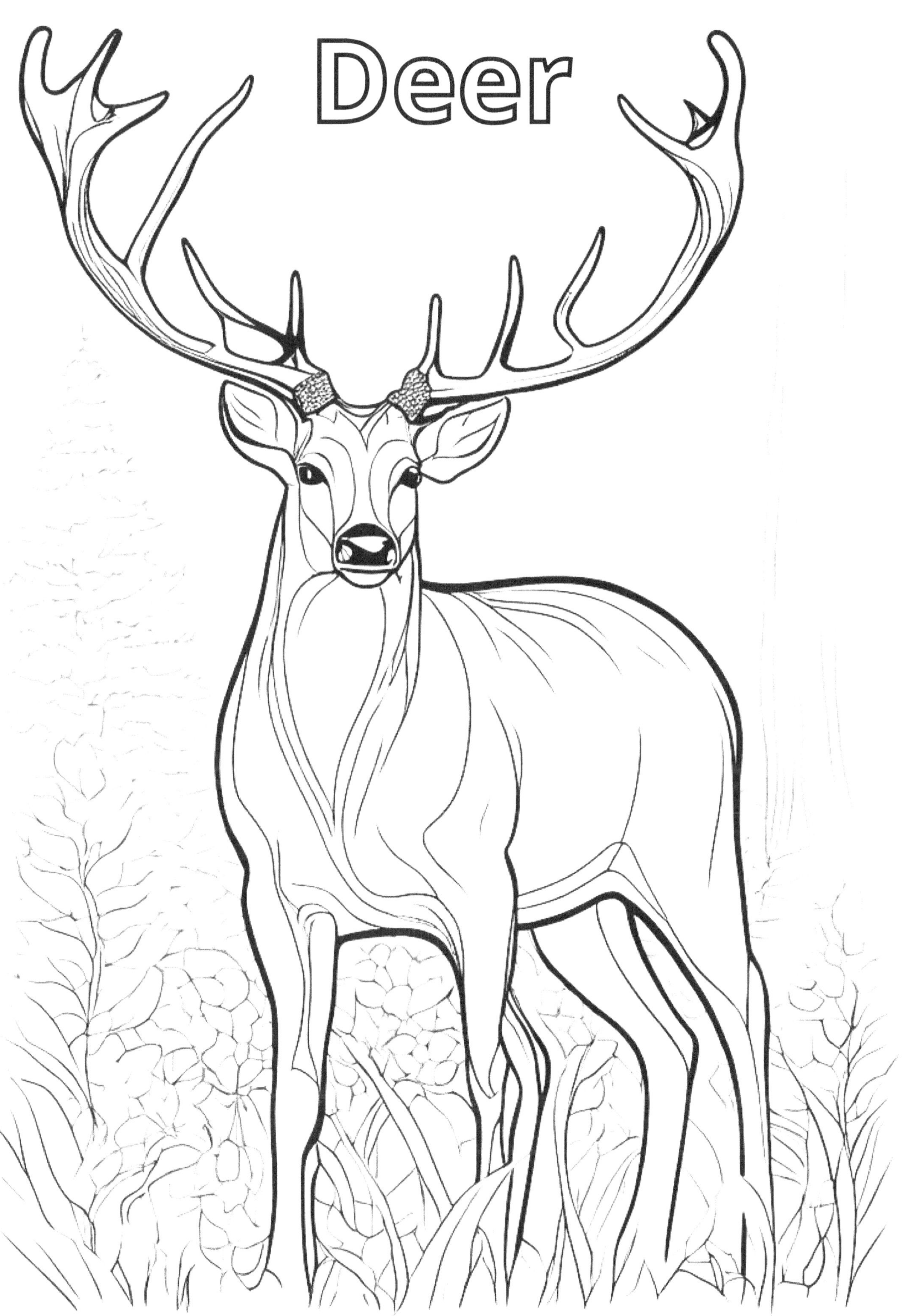

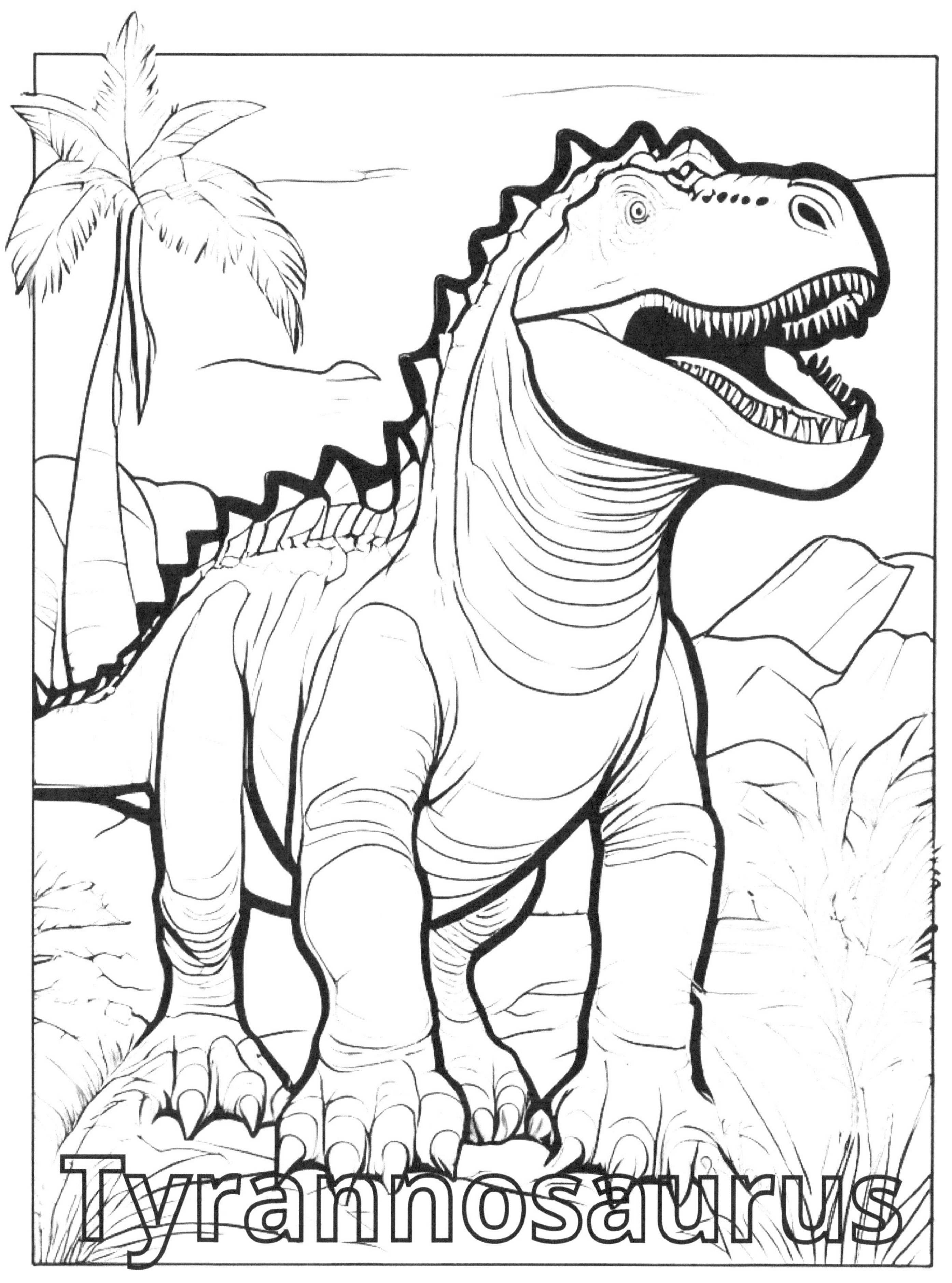
Tyrannosaurus

Duckling

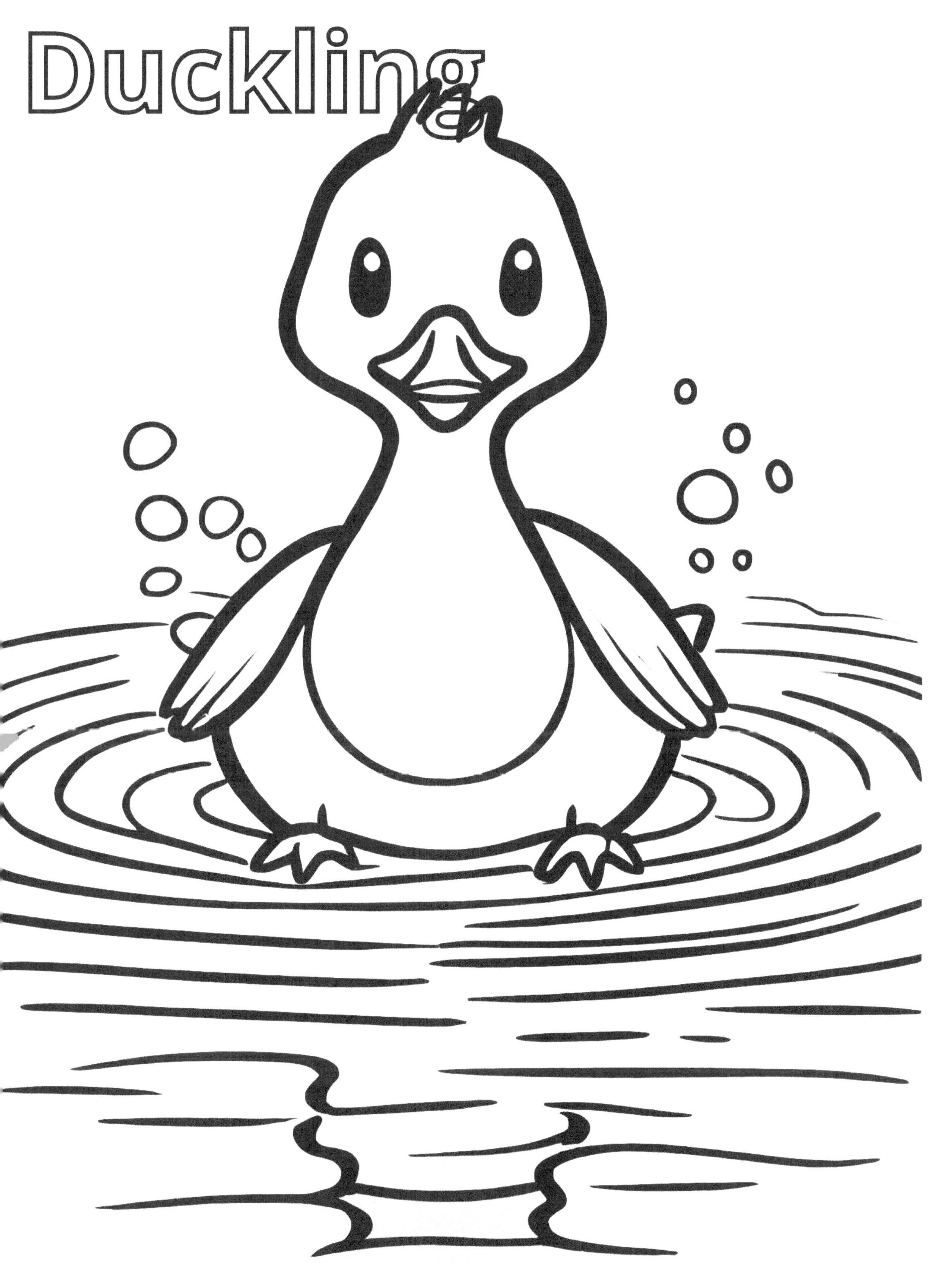

Penguin

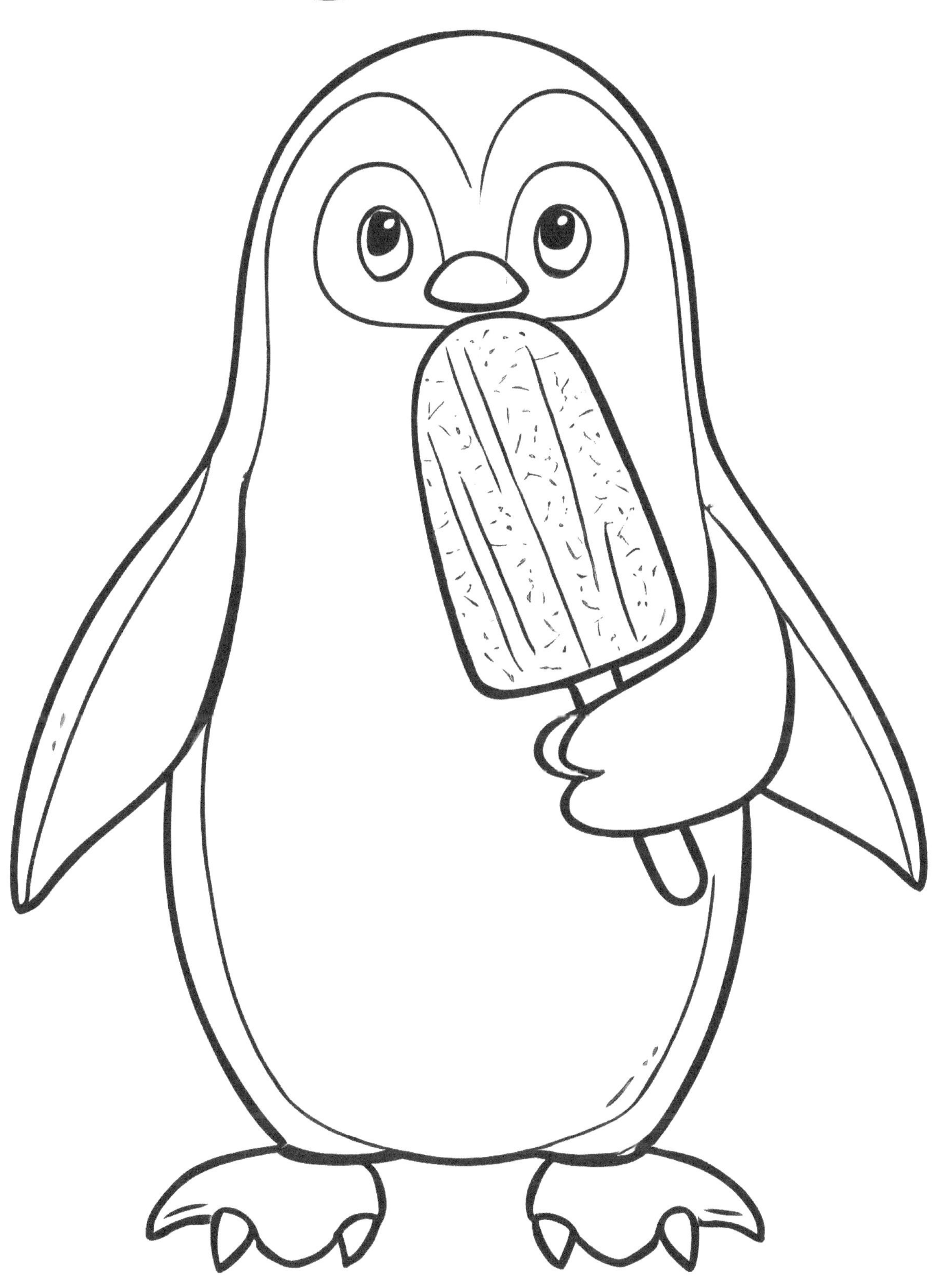

Fish

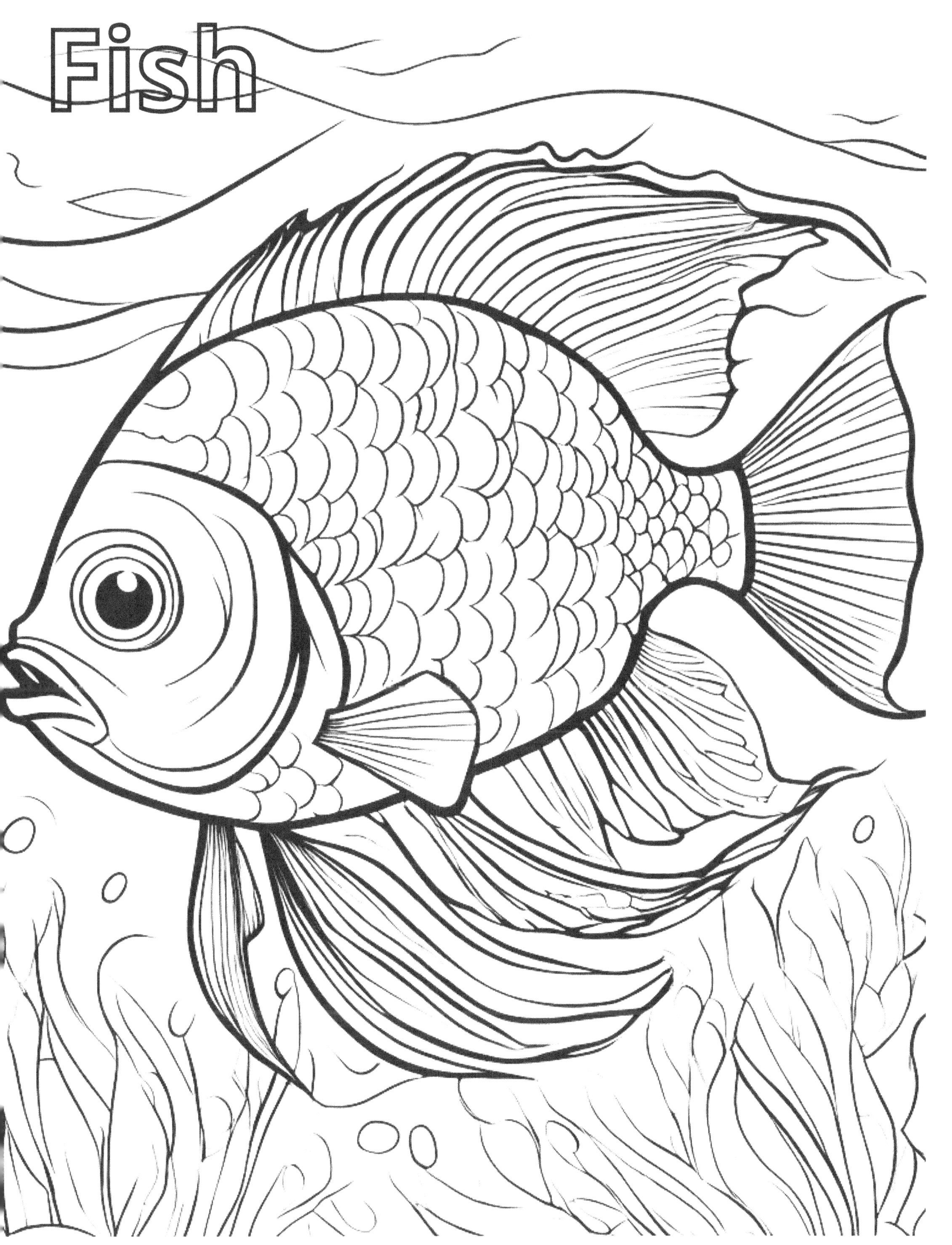

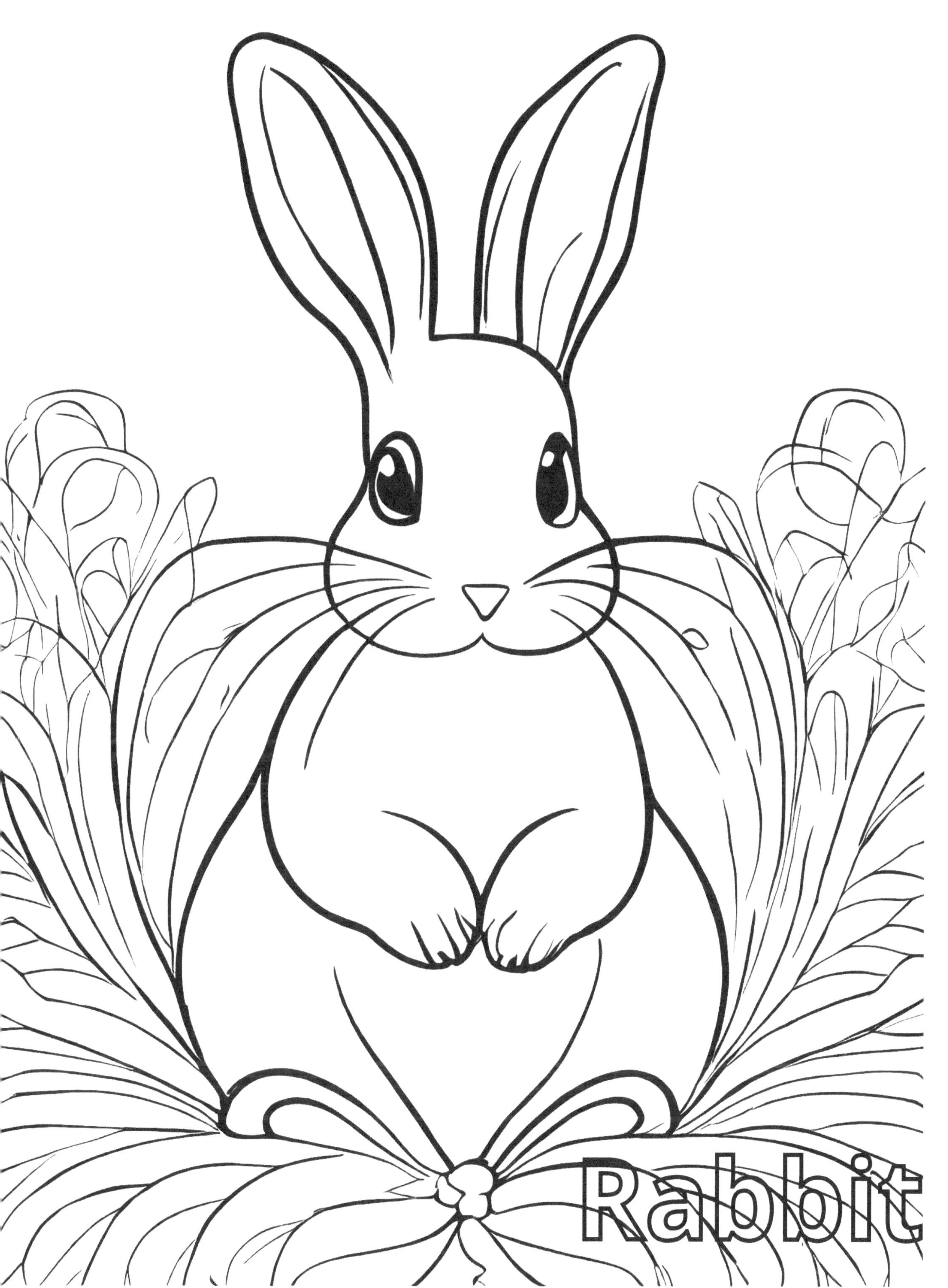

Rabbit

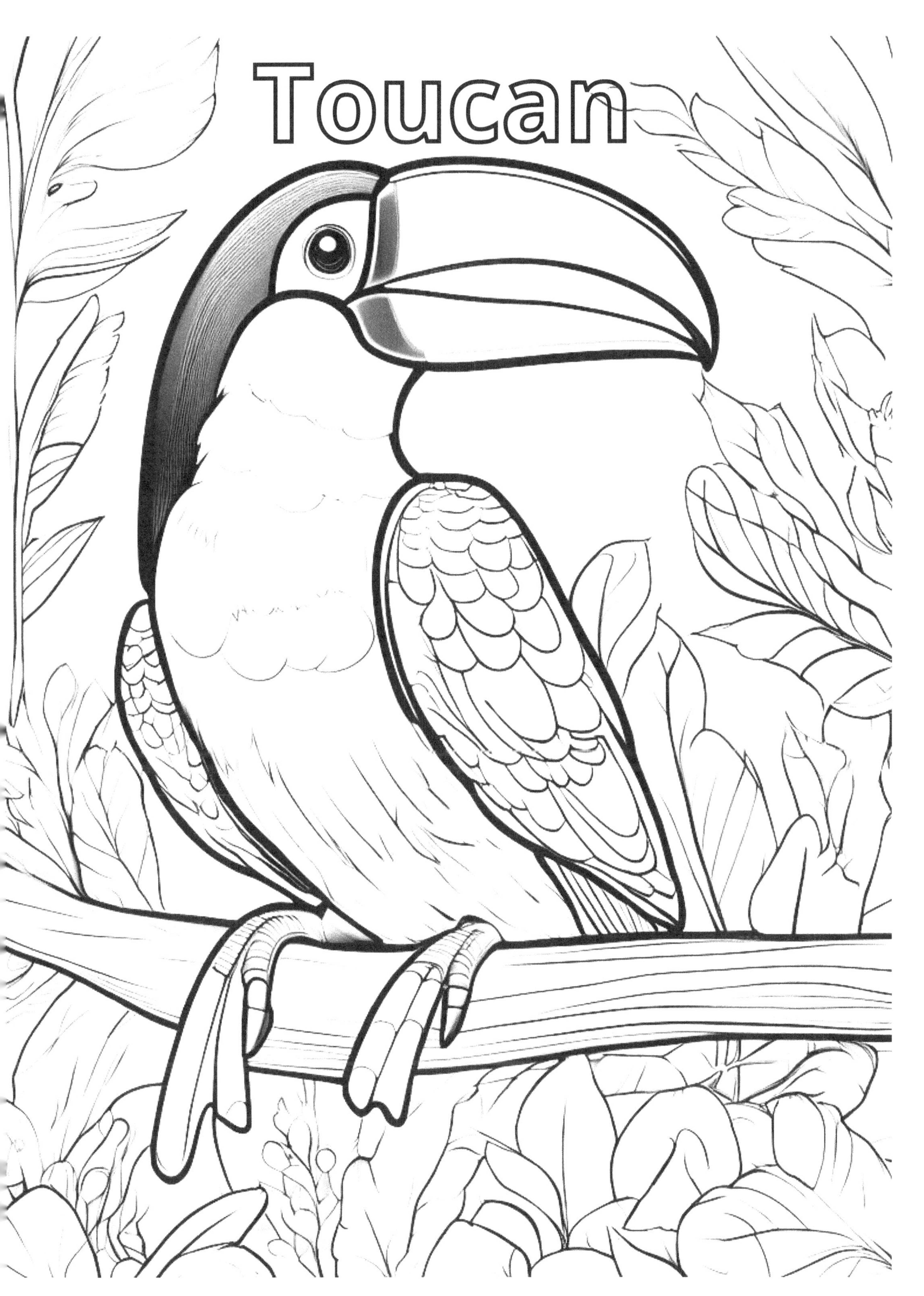
Toucan

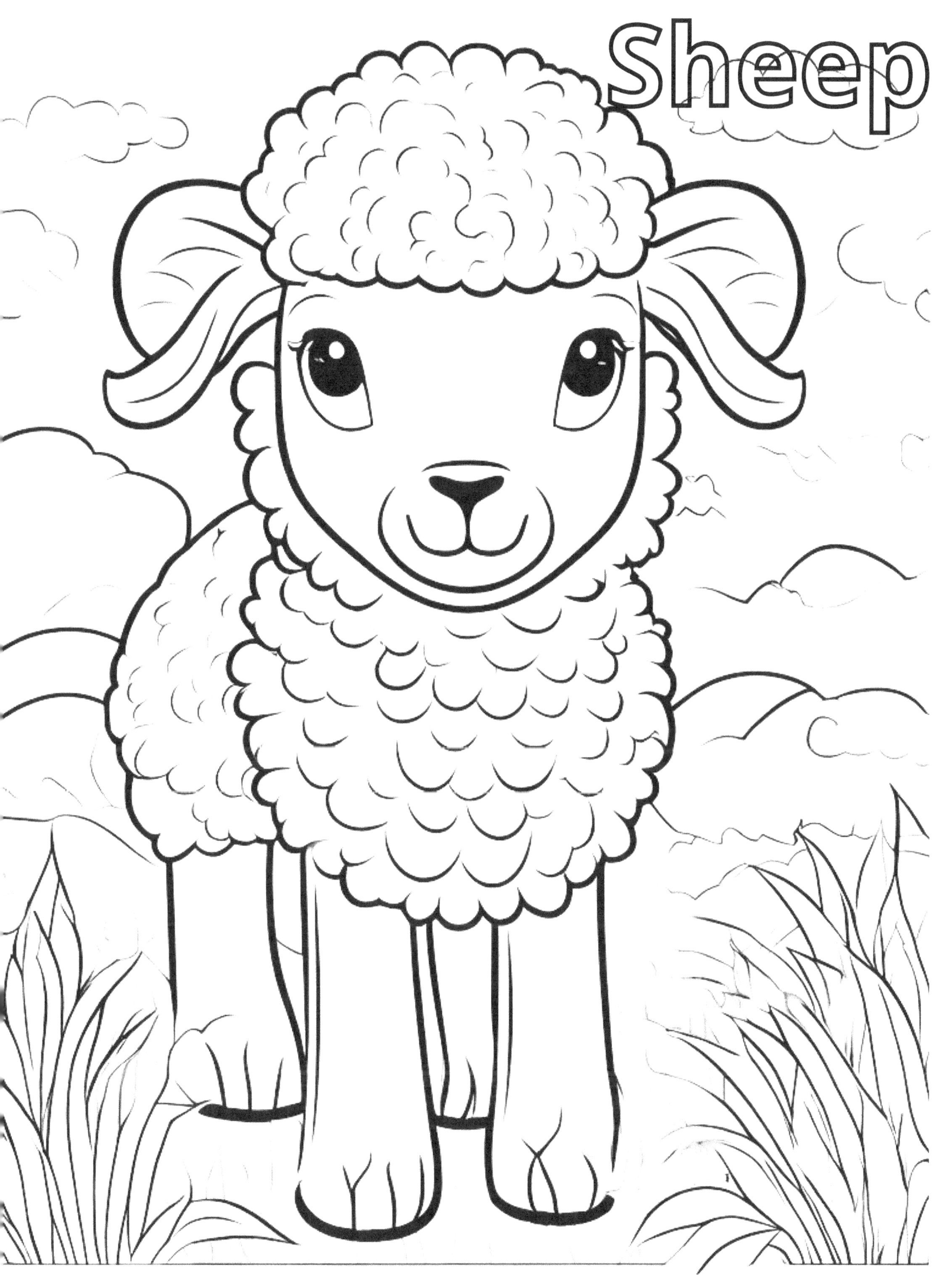
Sheep